KT-168-011

THE THEATER OF THE
BAUHAUS

WITHDRAWN FROM
THE LIBRARY

UNIVERSITY OF
WINCHESTER

KA 0218411 7

PAJ BOOKS • BONNIE MARRANCA AND GAUTAM DASGUPTA, SERIES EDITORS

From The Figural Cabinet by Oskar Schlemmer.
Technical production: Carl Schlemmer.
Production with music by G. Münch-Dresden in preparation. (Figures patented.)

Photograph: Strauch-Halle.

OSKAR SCHLEMMER • LASZLO
MOHOLY-NAGY • FARKAS MOLNÁR

THE THEATER
OF THE
BAUHAUS

Edited by

WALTER GROPIUS
AND ARTHUR S. WENSINGER

Translated by

ARTHUR S. WENSINGER

THE JOHNS HOPKINS UNIVERSITY PRESS
BALTIMORE AND LONDON

KING ALFRED'S COLLEGE
WINCHESTER

792.143GRO 02184117

Copyright © 1961 by Wesleyan University
All rights reserved
Printed in the United States of America on acid-free paper

Originally published in the United States by Wesleyan University Press, 1961
Johns Hopkins Paperbacks edition, 1996
06 05 04 03 02 01 00 99 98 97 96   5 4 3 2 1

The Johns Hopkins University Press
2715 North Charles Street
Baltimore, Maryland 21218-4319
The Johns Hopkins Press Ltd., London

Library of Congress Cataloging-in Publication Data
Schlemmer, Oskar, 1888–1943.
  [Bühne im Bauhaus.   English]
  The theater of the Bauhaus / Oskar Schlemmer, László Moholy-Nagy, Farkas Molnar ; edited
by Walter Gropius ; translated by Arthur S. Wensinger.
      p.   cm. — (PAJ books)
  Originally published: Middletown, Conn. : Wesleyan University, 1961.
  ISBN 0–8018–5528–4 (alk. paper)
  1. Theaters—Stage-setting and scenery.   2. Costume.   3. Bauhaus.
I. Moholy-Nagy, László, 1895–1946.   II. Molnár, Farkas.   III. Title.   IV. Series.
PN2091.S8S3313   1996
792'.025—dc20
                                                                                96–33458
                                                                                CIP

Statements by T. Lux Feininger are quoted from his article "The Bauhaus: Evolution of an Idea,"
Criticism, II, 3 (Summer 1960), pp. 261, 272–274; copyright © 1960 by the Wayne State
University Press; reprinted by permission of the author and the Wayne State University Press.

A catalog record for this book is available from the British Library.

CONTENTS

1

WALTER GROPIUS

INTRODUCTION

During the all too few years of its existence, the Bauhaus embraced the whole range of visual arts: architecture, planning, painting, sculpture, industrial design, and stage work. The aim of the Bauhaus was to find a new and powerful working correlation of all the processes of artistic creation to culminate finally in a new cultural equilibrium of our visual environment. This could not be achieved by individual withdrawal into an ivory tower. Teachers and students as a working community had to become vital participants of the modern world, seeking a new synthesis of art and modern technology. Based on the study of the biological facts of human perception, the phenomena of form and space were investigated in a spirit of unbiased curiosity, to arrive at objective means with which to relate individual creative effort to a common background. One of the fundamental maxims of the Bauhaus was the demand that the teacher's own approach was never to be imposed on the student; that, on the contrary, any attempt at imitation by the student was to be ruthlessly suppressed. The stimulation received from the teacher was only to help him find his own bearings.

This book gives evidence of the Bauhaus approach in the specific field of stage work. Here Oskar Schlemmer played a unique role within the community of the Bauhaus. When he joined the staff in 1921, he first headed the sculpture workshop. But step by step, out of his own initiative, he broadened the scope of this workshop and developed it into the Bauhaus stage shop, which became a splendid place of learning. I gave this stage shop wider and wider range within the Bauhaus curriculum since it attracted students from all departments and workshops. They became fascinated by the creative attitude of their Master Magician.

The most characteristic artistic quality in Oskar Schlemmer's work is his interpretation of space. From his paintings, as well as from his stage work for ballet and theater, it is apparent that he experienced space not only through mere vision but with the whole body, with the sense of touch of the dancer and the actor.

He transformed into abstract terms of geometry or mechanics his observation of the human figure moving in space. His figures and forms are pure creations of imagination, symbolizing eternal types of human character and their different moods, serene or tragic, funny or serious.

Possessed with the idea of finding new symbols, he considered it a "mark of Cain in our culture that we have no symbols any more and — worse — that we are unable to create them." Endowed with the power of genius to penetrate beyond rational thought, he found images which expressed metaphysical ideas, e.g. the star form of the spread-out fingers of the hand, the sign of infinity ∞ of "the folded arms." The mask of disguise, forgotten on the stage of realism since the theater of the Greeks and used today only in the No theater of Japan which — as we believe — Schlemmer did not know, became a stage tool of great importance in Schlemmer's hands. I want to quote a vivid and characteristic report of a Bauhaus pupil of Schlemmer's, T. Lux Feininger, who saw "with breathless excitement, admiration, and wonder an evening's performance of the stage class in the Bauhaus theater." He writes:

"At an early age I had occupied myself intensely with the making of masks in various materials, I hardly could say why, yet sensing dimly that in this form of creation a meaning lay hidden for me. On the Bauhaus stage, these intuitions seemed to acquire body and life. I had beheld the 'Dance of Gestures' and the 'Dance of Forms,' executed by dancers in metallic masks and costumed in padded, sculptural suits. The stage, with jet-black backdrop and wings, contained magically spotlighted, geometrical furniture: a cube, a white sphere, steps; the actors paced, strode, slunk, trotted, dashed, stopped short, turned slowly and majestically; arms with colored gloves were extended in a beckoning gesture; the copper and gold and silver heads . . . were laid together, flew apart; the silence was broken by a whirring sound, ending in a small thump; a crescendo of buzzing noises culminated in a crash followed by portentous and dismayed silence. Another phase of the dance had all the formal and contained violence of a chorus of cats, down to the meeowling and bass growls, which were marvellously accentuated by the resonant mask-heads. Pace and gesture, figure and prop, color and sound, all had the quality of elementary form, demonstrating anew the problem of the theatre of Schlemmer's concept: man in space. What we had seen had the significance of expounding the stage elements (*Die Bühnenelemente*). . . . The stage elements were assembled, re-grouped, amplified, and gradually grew into something like a 'play,' we never found out whether comedy or tragedy. . . . The interesting feature about it was that, with a set of formal elements agreed upon and, on this common basis, added to fairly freely by members of the class, 'play' with meaningful form was expected eventually to yield meaning, sense or message; that gestures and sounds would become speech and plot. Who knows? This was, essentially, a dancers' theatre and as such, sufficient unto itself as Oskar Schlemmer's genius had created it; but it was also a 'class,' a locale of learning, and this rather magnificent undertaking was Schlemmer's tool of instruction. . . .

"Indeed it was a treat to watch the precision, aplomb, the power and the delicacy of action. His language, too, although unable to assume command, was an expressive tool. His was the most personal vocabulary I have ever known. His invention of metaphors was inexhaustible; he loved unaccustomed juxtapositions, paradoxical alliterations, baroque hyperbole. The satirical wit of his writings is quite untranslatable."

Schlemmer's unorthodox approach to the phenomenon of creation, which expected form to yield meaning, has recently found an eloquent advocate in Sir Herbert Read, the English poet and art critic. He has devoted his book *Icon and Idea* to the question whether "image" or "thought" initiates a new phase of development in human history. He comes to the conclusion that it may well be that the formative artist receives the first message from beyond the threshold of knowledge, which is then interpreted by the thinker, the philosopher.

My own great impression of Schlemmer's stage work was to see and experience his magic of transforming dancers and actors into moving architecture. His deep interest and intuitive understanding of the phenomena of architectural space developed also his rare gift as a muralist. With empathy he would sense the directions and dynamics of a given space and make them integral parts of his mural compositions — as, for instance, in the Bauhaus buildings in Weimar. His are the only murals of our time I know which offer a complete fusion and unity with architecture.

Oskar Schlemmer's literary bequest, particularly his chapter on "Mensch und Kunstfigur," the principal article of this book, is classic in form and content. In it he offers basic values for stage art cast in a beautiful and concise language, reinforced by illustrations and diagrams in his unique handwriting. Such clarity and control of thought, reaching universal and timeless validity, mark a man of vision.

From quite a different angle came the contribution of Laszlo Moholy-Nagy to the Bauhaus stage. Originally an abstract painter, his inner urge caused him to penetrate into many fields of artistic design: typography, advertising art, photography, film, theater. He was a man of fiery spirit, full of vitality, love, and contagious enthusiasm. The aim of his creations was to observe "vision in motion" in order to find a new space conception. Entirely unprejudiced by conventional methods, he ventured into ever new experiments with the curiosity of a scientist. In order to enrich visual representation, he applied new materials and new mechanical means to his work. His article in this book, "Theater, Circus, Variety," gives evidence of his exuberant imagination. With it is included his "Score Sketch for Mechanized Eccentric" for the stage, which offers a synthesis of form, motion, sound, light, color, and scent.

Out of his theoretical laboratory experiments in the Bauhaus, Moholy later developed original stage settings for the Kroll Opera House in Berlin for the *Tales of Hoffmann* and for other operatic and theatrical performances which brought him fame as a stage designer between the two world wars.

Those years in the Bauhaus were a period of mutual stimulation. I myself felt that the modern stage and theater which would do justice to these new interpretations of theatrical space was still to be created. The opportunity arrived with the performances of Erwin Piscator in Berlin in 1926, for whom I designed the "Total Theater," the building of which had to be abandoned after the German "Black Friday" shortly before Hitler and the Nazis took over the government of Germany.

At the "Volta Congress" in Rome on the "Teatro Dramatico" in 1935, I

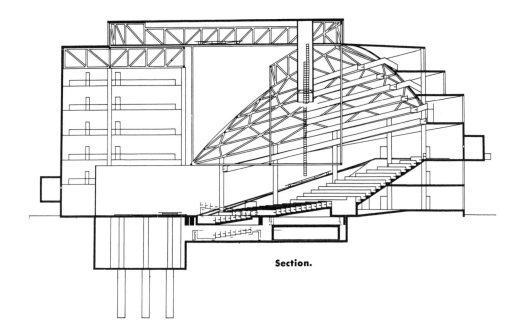

Section.

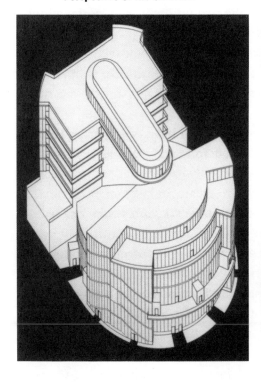

Perspective of the exterior.

View into the auditorium (model).

presented this project to an international gathering of writers and theater producers with these explanations:

"The contemporary theater architect should set himself the aim to create a great keyboard for light and space, so objective and adaptable in character that it would respond to any imaginable vision of a stage director; a flexible building, capable of transforming and refreshing the mind by its spatial impact alone.

"There are only three basic stage forms in existence. The primary one is the central arena on which the play unfolds itself three-dimensionally while the spectators crowd around concentrically. Today we know this form only as a circus, a bull ring, or a sports arena.

"The second classic stage form is the Greek proscenium theater with its protruding platform around which the audience is seated in concentric half-circles. Here the play is set up against a fixed background like a relief.

"Eventually this open proscenium receded more and more from the spectator, to be finally pulled back altogether behind a curtain to form today's deep stage which dominates our present theater.

"Much as the spatial separation of the two different worlds, the auditorium and the stage, has helped to bring about technical progress, it fails to draw the spectator physically into the orbit of the play; being on the other side of the curtain or the orchestra pit, he remains beside the drama, not in it. The theater is thereby robbed of one of its strongest means to make the spectator participate in the drama.

"Some people believe that film and television have eclipsed the theater altogether, but is it not its present limited form only which is becoming obsolete, not the theater as such?

"In my Total Theater . . . I have tried to create an instrument so flexible that a director can employ any one of the three stage forms by the use of simple, ingenious mechanisms. The expenditure for such an interchangeable stage mechanism would be fully compensated for by the diversity of purposes to which such a building would lend itself: for presentation of drama, opera, film, and dance; for choral or instrumental music; for sports events or assemblies. Conventional plays could be just as easily accommodated as the most fantastic experimental creations of a stage director of the future.

"An audience will shake off its inertia when it experiences the surprise effect of space transformed. By shifting the scene of action during the per-

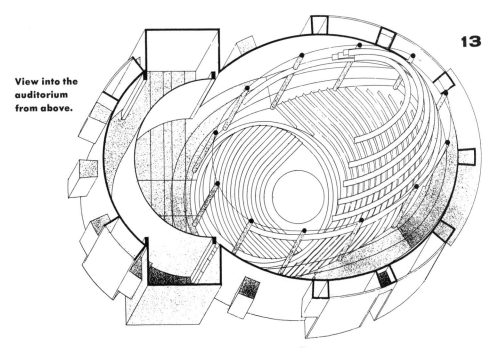

View into the
auditorium
from above.

PLANS AND MODEL OF THE SYNTHETIC "TOTAL THEATER," 1926

This theater provides a stage in arena form, a proscenium and a back stage, the latter divided in three parts. The 2,000 seats are disposed in the form of an amphitheater. There are no boxes. By turning the big stage platform which is solidary with part of the orchestra, the small proscenium stage is placed in the center of the theater, and the usual set can be replaced by projecting scenery on twelve screens placed between the twelve main columns supporting the structure.

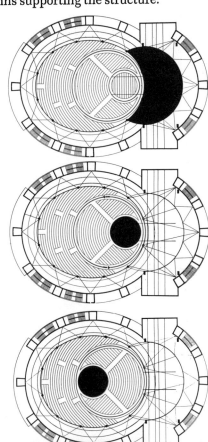

Plan showing the use of the deep stage.

Plan showing the use of the proscenium stage.

Plan showing the use of the center stage.

formance from one stage position to another and by using a system of spotlights and film projectors, transforming walls and ceiling into moving picture
scenes, the whole house would be animated by three-dimensional means
instead of by the 'flat' picture effect of the customary stage. This would also
greatly reduce the cumbersome paraphernalia of properties and painted
backdrops.

"Thus the playhouse itself, made to dissolve into the shifting, illusionary
space of the imagination, would become the scene of action itself. Such a
theater would stimulate the conception and fantasy of playwright and stage
director alike; for if it is true that the mind can transform the body, it is
equally true that structure can transform the mind."

Cambridge, Mass., June 1961

OSKAR SCHLEMMER
MAN AND ART FIGURE

OSKAR SCHLEMMER
MAN AND ART FIGURE

The history of the theater is the history of the transfiguration of the human form. It is the history of *man* as the actor of physical and spiritual events, ranging from naïveté to reflection, from naturalness to artifice.

The materials involved in this transfiguration are form and color, the materials of the painter and sculptor. The arena for this transfiguration is found in the constructive fusion of *space and building*, the realm of the architect. Through the manipulation of these materials the role of the artist, the synthesizer of these elements, is determined.

One of the emblems of our time is *abstraction*. It functions, on the one hand, to disconnect components from an existing and persisting whole, either to lead them individually *ad absurdum* or to elevate them to their greatest potential. On the other hand, abstraction can result in generalization and summation, in the construction in bold outline of a new totality.

A further emblem of our time is *mechanization*, the inexorable process which now lays claim to every sphere of life and art. Everything which can be mechanized *is* mechanized. The result: our recognition of that which can *not* be mechanized.

And last, but not the least, among the emblems of our time are the new potentials of technology and invention which we can use to create altogether new hypotheses and which can thus engender, or at least give promise of, the boldest fantasies.

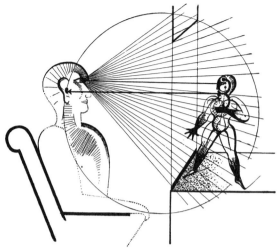

The theater, which should be the image of our time and perhaps the one art form most peculiarly conditioned by it, must not ignore these signs.

Stage (*Bühne*), taken in its general sense, is what we may call the entire realm lying between religious cult and naïve popular entertainment. Neither of these things, however, is really the same thing as stage. Stage is *representation* abstracted from the natural and directing its effect at the human being.

This confrontation of passive spectator and animate actor preconditions also the form of the stage, at its most monumental as the antique arena and at its most primitive as the scaffold in the market place. The need for concentration resulted in the peep show or "picture frame," today the "universal" form of the stage. The term *theater* designates the most basic nature of the stage: make-believe, mummery, metamorphosis. Between cult and theater lies "the stage seen as a moral institution"; between theater and popular entertainment lie variety (vaudeville) and circus: the stage as an institution for the artiste. (See accompanying diagram.)

The question as to the origin of life and the cosmos, that is, whether in the beginning there was Word, Deed, or Form — Spirit, Act, or Shape — Mind, Happening, or Manifestation — pertains also to the world of the stage, and leads us to a differentiation of:

> the *oral or sound stage* (*Sprech-oder Tonbühne*) of a literary or musical event;
>
> the *play stage* (*Spielbühne*) of a physical-mimetic event;
>
> the *visual stage* (*Schaubühne*) of an optical event.

SCHEME FOR STAGE, CULT, AND POPULAR ENTERTAINMENT ACCORDING TO:

PLACE	PERSON	GENRE	SPEECH	MUSIC	DANCE
TEMPLE	PRIEST		SERMON	ORATORIO	DERVISH
ARCHITECTUAL STAGE	PROPHET		ANCIENT TRAGEDY	EARLY OPERA (e.g. Handel)	MASS GYMNASTICS
STYLIZED OR SPACE STAGE	SPEAKER		SCHILLER ("BRIDE OF MESSINA")	WAGNER	CHORIC DANCE
THEATER OF ILLUSION	ACTOR		SHAKESPEARE	MOZART	BALLET
WINGS AND BORDERS	PERFORMER (COMMEDIAN)		IMPROVISA—TION COMMEDIA DELL'ARTE	OPERA BUFFA OPERETTA	MIME & MUMMERY
SIMPLEST STAGE OR APPARATUS & MACHINERY	ARTISTE		CONFERENCIER (M.C.)	MUSIC HALL SONG JAZZ BAND	CARICATURE & PARODY
PODIUM SCAFFOLD	ARTISTE		CLOWNERY	CIRCUS BAND	ACROBATICS
FAIRGROUND SIDESHOW	FOOL JESTER		DOGGEREL BALLAD	FOLK SONG	FOLK DANCE

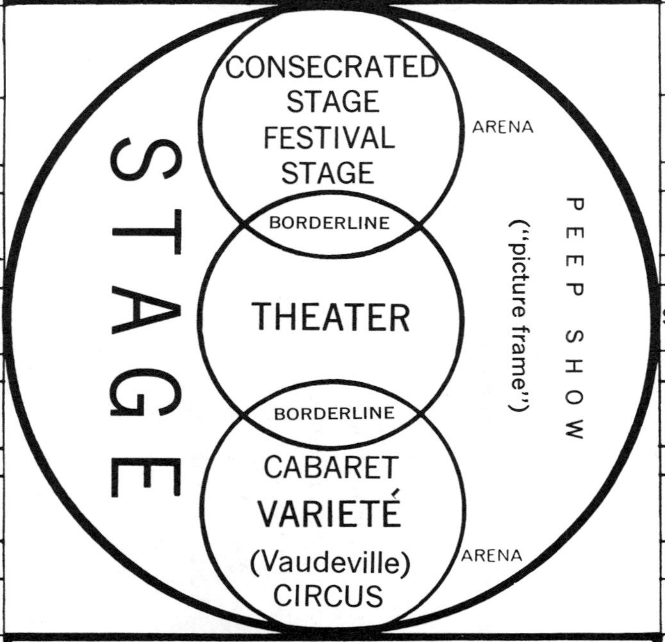

GENRE column (central diagram):

RELIGIOUS CULT ACTIVITY

FOLK ENTERTAINMENT

STAGE

PEEP SHOW ("picture frame")

ARENA — BORDERLINE — BORDERLINE — ARENA

CONSECRATED STAGE / FESTIVAL STAGE — THEATER — CABARET / VARIETÉ (Vaudeville) / CIRCUS

Each of these stage forms has its corresponding representative, thus:

the *author* (as writer or composer) who is the creator of the word or musical sound;

the *actor* whose body and its movements make him the player;

the *designer* who is the builder of form and color.

Each of these stage forms can exist for itself and be complete within itself.

The combination of two or all three stage forms — with one of them always predominating — is a question of weight distribution, and is something that can be perfected with mathematical precision. The executor of this process is the universal *regisseur* or *director*. E.g.:

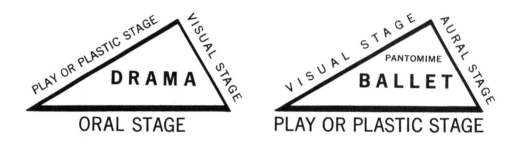

From the standpoint of *material* the actor has the advantages of immediacy and independence. He constitutes his own material with his body, his voice, his gestures, and his movements. Today, however, the once noble type who was both the poet and the projector of his own word has become an ideal. At one time Shakespeare, who was an actor before he was a poet, filled this role — so, too, did the improvising actors of the *commedia dell' arte*. Today's actor bases his existence as player on the writer's word. Yet when the word is silent, when the body alone is articulate and its play is on exhibition — as a dancer's is — then it is free and is its own lawgiver.

The material of the author is *word or sound.*

Except for the unusual circumstance in which he is his own actor, singer, or musician, he creates the representational material for transmission and reproduction on the stage, whether it is meant for the organic human voice or for artificial, abstract instruments. The higher the state of perfection of the latter, the broader their formative potential, while the human voice is and remains a limited, if unique, phenomenon. Mechanical reproduction by means of various kinds of technological equipment is now capable of replacing the sound of the musical instrument and the human voice or of detaching it from its source, and can enlarge it beyond its dimensional and temporal limitations.

The material of the formative artist — painter, sculptor, architect — is *form and color.*

These formative means, invented by the human mind, can be called *abstract* by virtue of their artificiality and insofar as they represent an undertaking whose purpose, contrary to nature, is order. Form is manifest in extensions of height, breadth, and depth; as line, as plane, and as solid or volume. Depending on these extensions, form becomes then linear framework, wall, or space, and, as such, rigid — i.e., tangible — form.

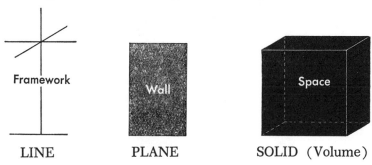

LINE   PLANE   SOLID (Volume)

Non-rigid, intangible form occurs as light, whose linear effect appears in the geometry of the light beam and of pyrotechnical display, and whose solid- and space-creating effect comes through illumination.

To each of these manifestations of light (which in themselves are already colored — only nothingness is without color) can be added *coloring* (*intensifying*) *color*.

Color and form reveal their elementary values within the constructive manipulation of architectonic space. Here they constitute both object and receptacle, that which is to be filled and fulfilled by Man, the living organism.

In painting and sculpture, form and color are the means of establishing these connections with organic nature through the representation of its phenomena. Man, its chief phenomenon, is both an organism of flesh and blood and at the same time the exponent of number and "Measure of All Things" (the Golden Section).

These arts — architecture, sculpture, painting — are fixed. They are momentary, frozen motion. Their nature is the immutability of not an accidental but a typified condition, the stability of forces in equilibrium. And thus what may appear at first as a deficiency, particularly in our age of motion, is actually their greatest merit.

The stage as the arena for successive and transient action, however, offers *form and color in motion,* in the first instance in their primary aspect as separate and individual mobile, colored or uncolored, linear, flat, or plastic forms, but furthermore as fluctuating, mobile space and as transformable architectonic structures. Such kaleidoscopic play, at once infinitely variable and strictly organized, would constitute — theoretically — the *absolute* visual stage (*Schaubühne*). Man, the animated being, would be banned from view in this mechanistic organism. He would stand as "the perfect engineer" at the central switchboard, from where he would direct this feast for the eyes.

Yet all the while Man seeks *meaning*. Whether it is the Faustian problem whose goal is the creation of Homunculus or the anthropomorphic impulse in Man which created his gods and idols, he is incessantly seeking his likeness, his image, or the sublime. He seeks his equal, the superman, or the figures of his fancy.

Man, the human organism, stands in the cubical, abstract space of the stage. Man and Space. Each has different laws of order. Whose shall prevail?

Either abstract space is adapted in deference to natural man and transformed back into nature or the imitation of nature. This happens in the theater of illusionistic realism.

Or natural man, in deference to abstract space, is recast to fit its mold. This happens on the abstract stage.

The laws of cubical space are the invisible linear network of planimetric and stereometric relationships. (See above sketch.) This mathematic corresponds to the inherent mathematic of the human body and creates its balance by means of movements, which by their very nature are determined *mechanically and rationally*. It is the geometry of calisthenics, eurhythmics, and gymnastics. These involve the *physical attributes* (together with facial stereotypy) which find expression in acrobatic precision and in the mass calisthenics of the stadium, although there is no conscious awareness of spatial relationships here. (See first sketch next page.)

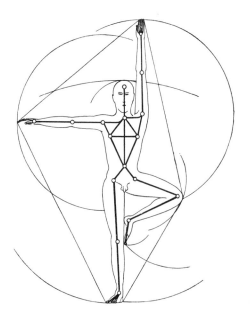

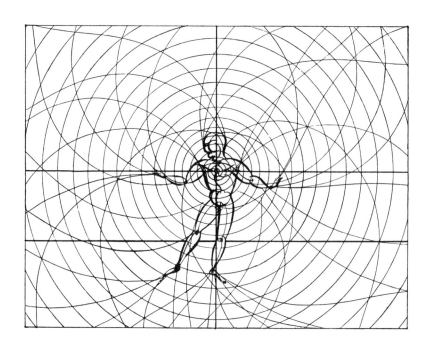

The laws of organic man, on the other hand, reside in the invisible functions of his inner self: heartbeat, circulation, respiration, the activities of the brain and nervous system. If these are to be the determining factors, then their center is the human being, whose movements and emanations create an imaginary space. (See bottom sketch opposite.) Cubical-abstract space is then only the horizontal and vertical framework for this flow. These movements are *determined organically and emotionally.* They constitute the *psychical impulses* (together with the mimetics of the face), which find expression in the great actor and in the mass scenes of great tragedy.

Invisibly involved with all these laws is Man as Dancer (Tänzermensch). *He obeys the law of the body as well as the law of space; he follows his sense of himself as well as his sense of embracing space.* As the one who gives birth to an almost endless range of expression, whether in free abstract movement or in symbolic pantomime, whether he is on the bare stage or in a scenic environment constructed for him, whether he speaks or sings, whether he is naked or costumed, the *Tänzermensch* is the medium of transition into the great world of the theater (*das grosse theatralische Geschehen*). Only one branch of this world, the metamorphosis of the human figure and its abstraction, is to be outlined here.

●

The transformation of the human body, its metamorphosis, is made possible by the *costume*, the disguise. Costume and mask emphasize the body's identity or they change it; they express its nature or they are purposely misleading about it; they stress its conformity to organic or mechanical laws or they invalidate this conformity.

The native costume, as produced by the conventions of religion, state, and society, is different from the theatrical stage costume. Yet the two are generally confused. Great as has been the variety of native costumes developed during the course of human history, the number of genuine stage costumes has stayed very small. They are the few standardized costumes of the *commedia dell' arte*: Harlequin, Pierrot, Columbine, etc.; and they have remained basic and authentic to this day.

The following can be considered fundamentally decisive in the transformation of the human body in terms of this stage costume:

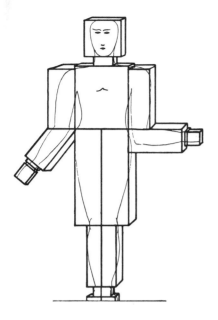

The laws of the surrounding cubical space. Here the cubical forms are transferred to the human shape: head, torso, arms, legs are transformed into spatial-cubical constructions.

Result: *ambulant architecture.*

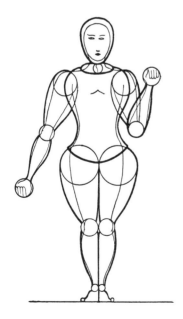

The functional laws of the human body in their relationship to space. These laws bring about a typification of the bodily forms: the egg shape of the head, the vase shape of the torso, the club shape of the arms and legs, the ball shape of the joints.

Result: *the marionette.*

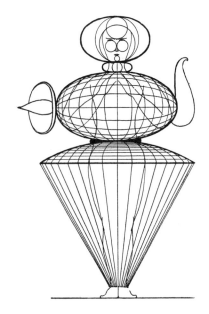

The laws of motion of the human body in space. Here we have the various aspects of rotation, direction, and intersection of space: the spinning top, snail, spiral, disk. Result: *a technical organism.*

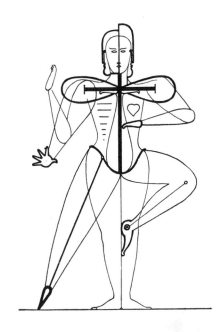

The metaphysical forms of expression symbolizing various members of the human body: the star shape of the spread hand, the ∞ sign of the folded arms, the cross shape of the backbone and shoulders; the double head, multiple limbs, division and suppression of forms. Result: *dematerialization.*

28

These are the possibilities of Man as Dancer, transformed through costume and moving in space. Yet there is no costume which can suspend the primary limitation of the human form: the law of gravity, to which it is subject. A step is not much longer than a yard, a leap not much higher than two. The center of gravity can be abandoned only momentarily. And only for a second can it endure in a position essentially alien to its natural one, such as a horizontal hovering or soaring.

Acrobatics make it possible to partially overcome physical limitations, though only in the realm of the organic: the contortionist with his double joints, the living geometry of the aerialist, the pyramid of human bodies.

The endeavor to free man from his physical bondage and to heighten his freedom of movement beyond his native potential resulted in substituting for the organism the mechanical human figure (*Kunstfigur*): *the automaton and the marionette.* E. T. A. Hoffmann extolled the first of these, Heinrich von Kleist the second.[1]

The English stage reformer Gordon Craig demands: "The actor must go, and in his place comes the inanimate figure — the Übermarionette we may call him."[2] And the Russian Brjusov demands that we "replace actors with mechanized dolls, into each of which a phonograph shall be built."

Such, indeed, are two actual conclusions arrived at by the stage designer whose mind is constantly concerned with form and transformation, with figure and configuration. As far as the stage is concerned, such paradoxical exclusiveness is less significant than the enrichment of modes of expression which is brought about by it.

Possibilities are extraordinary in light of today's technological advancements: precision machinery, scientific apparatus of glass and metal, the

---

[1] Schlemmer's reference to the automaton is based on the story *Der Sandmann* from the *Nachtstücke* of E. T. A. Hoffmann (1776–1822), where appear the mad physics professor Spalanzani and his "daughter" Olimpia, a machine. The characters were also used by Jacques Offenbach in his *Tales of Hoffmann* (1881). The second reference is to Heinrich von Kleist's (1777–1811) famous little essay *Über das Marionettentheater,* a philosophical speculation on the essence and aesthetic implications for man of the free and "anti-grave" marionette. The essay is available in a translation by Eugene Jolas as "Essay on the Puppet Theater," *Partisan Review,* XIV (1943), 67–74. (Translator)

[2] Schlemmer quotes (Edward) Gordon Craig (1872–   ) exactly; the latter speaks of an "Übermarionette" in his *On the Art of the Theatre* (Chicago, Browne, 1911), p. 81. (Translator)

artificial limbs developed by surgery, the fantastic costumes of the deep-sea diver and the modern soldier, and so forth. . . .

Consequently, potentialities of constructive configuration are extraordinary on the metaphysical side as well.

The artificial human figure (*Kunstfigur*) permits any kind of movement and any kind of position for as long a time as desired. It also permits — an artistic device from the periods of greatest art — a variable relative scale for figures: important ones can be large, unimportant ones small.

An equally significant aspect of this is the possibility of relating the figure of natural "naked" Man to the abstract figure, both of which experience, through this confrontation, an intensification of their peculiar natures.

Endless perspectives are opened up: from the supernatural to the nonsensical, from the sublime to the comic. Precursors in the use of pathos, of the sublime, are the actors of ancient tragedy, monumentalized by means of masks, cothurni, and stilts. Precursors in the comic style are the gigantic and the grotesque figures of carnival and fair.

Wondrous figures of this new sort, personifications of the loftiest concepts and ideas, made of the most exquisite material, will be capable also of embodying symbolically a new faith.

Seen from this perspective, it might even be predicted that the situation will completely reverse itself: the stage designer will develop optical phenomena and will then seek out a poet who will give them their appropriate language through words and musical sounds.

And so, in accordance with idea, style, and technology, the following still await their creation:

the Abstract-Formal and Color	
the Static, Dynamic, and Tectonic	
the Mechanical, Automatic, and Electric	
the Gymnastic, Acrobatic, and Equilibristic	Theater
the Comic, Grotesque, and Burlesque	
the Serious, Sublime, and Monumental	
the Political, Philosophical, and Metaphysical	

●

Utopia? It is indeed astonishing how little has been accomplished so far in this direction. This materialistic and practical age has in fact lost the genuine

feeling for play and for the miraculous. Utilitarianism has gone a long way in killing it. Amazed at the flood of technological advance, we accept these wonders of utility as being already perfected art form, while actually they are only prerequisites for its creation. "Art is without purpose" insofar as the imaginary needs of the soul can be said to be without purpose. In this time of crumbling religion, which kills the sublime, and of a decaying society, which is able to enjoy only play that is drastically erotic or artistically *outré*, all profound artistic tendencies take on the character of exclusiveness or of sectarianism.

And so there remain only three possibilities for the artist in the theater today!

He may seek realization within the confines of the given situation. This means cooperation with the stage in its present form — productions in which he places himself at the service of writers and actors in order to give to their work the appropriate optical form. It is a rare case when his intentions coincide with those of the author.

Or he may seek realization under conditions of the greatest possible freedom. This exists for him in those areas of staging which are primarily visual display, where author and actor step back in favor of the optical or else achieve their effect only by virtue of it: ballet, pantomime, musical theater, and the like. It also exists in those areas — independent of writer and actor — of the anonymous or mechanically controlled play of forms, colors, and figures.

Or he may isolate himself altogether from the existing theater and cast his anchor far out into the sea of fantasy and distant possibilities. In this case his projects remain paper and model, materials for demonstration lectures

---

THE TWO SOLEMN TRAGEDIANS (*DIE BEIDEN PATHETIKER*) (working drawing.) Two monumental figures, proscenium height, personifications of lofty concepts such as Power and Courage, Truth and Beauty, Law and Freedom. Their dialog: voices amplified by megaphones proportionate to the size of the figures; fluctuating in volume, at certain times with orchestral accompaniment.

The figures — on wagons — are conceived as three-dimensional reliefs; cloth skirts trail behind upon entrance; masks and torsos of papier-mâché are covered with metallic foil; arms are hinged in order to make possible sparse and significant gestures.

By contrast, and to give the proper scale, there is natural man with his natural voice, moving about in the three zones of the stage (i.e., up, down, and center stage), establishing the dimensions vocally and physically.

and exhibitions of theater art. His plans founder on the impossibility of materialization. In the final analysis this is unimportant to him. His idea has been demonstrated, and its realization is a question of time, material, and technology. This realization will come with the construction of the new theater of glass, metal, and the inventions of tomorrow.

It depends as well upon the inner transformation of the spectator — Man as alpha and omega of every artistic creation which, even in its realization, is doomed to remain Utopia so long as it does not find intellectual and spiritual receptivity and response.

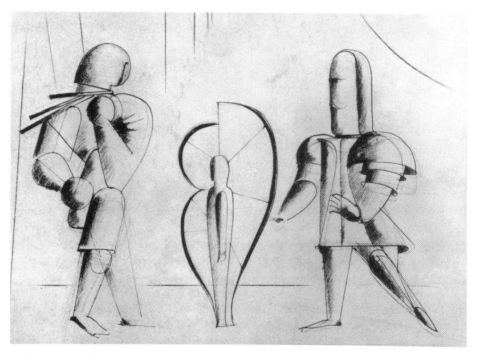

GRANDIOSE SCENE (sketch). Similar in intention to *Die beiden Pathetiker.* Two exaggerated heroes in metal armor; a female figure in glass.

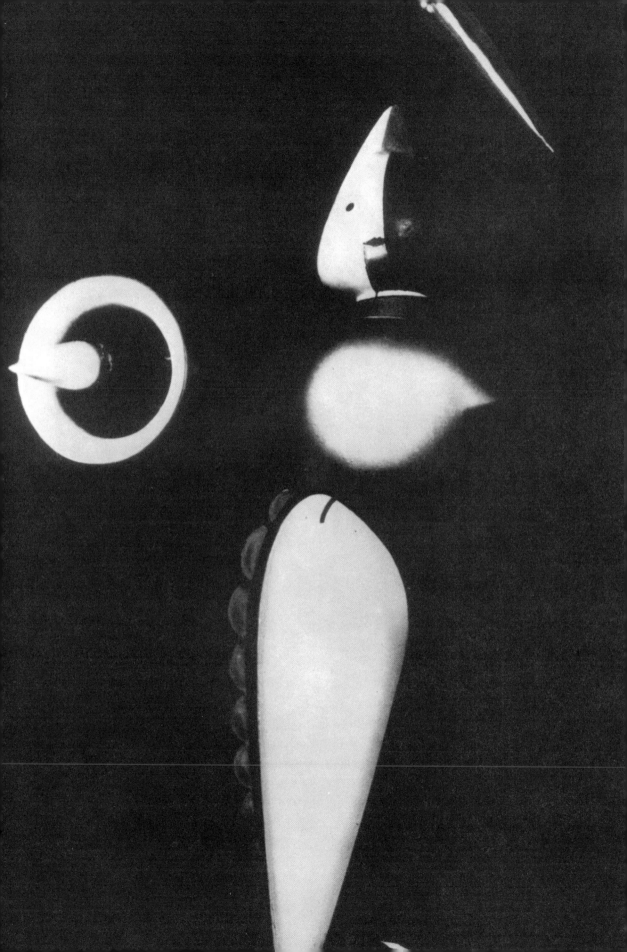

THE TRIADIC BALLET. (Originated 1912 in Stuttgart in cooperation with the dance team Albert Burger and Elsa Hötzel and the master craftsman Carl Schlemmer. First performance of parts of the ballet in 1915. First performance of the entire ballet September, 1922, in the Stuttgart Landestheater. Also performed in 1923 during the Bauhaus Week at the Nationaltheater, Weimar, and at the Annual Exhibition of German Crafts, Dresden.)

The Triadic Ballet consists of three parts which form a structure of stylized dance scenes, developing from the humorous to the serious. The first is a gay burlesque with lemon-yellow drop curtains. The second, ceremonious and solemn, is on a rose-colored stage. And the third is a mystical fantasy on a black stage. The twelve different dances in eighteen different costumes are danced alternately by three persons, two male and one female. The costumes are partly of padded cloth and partly of stiff papier-mâché forms, coated with metallic or colored paint.

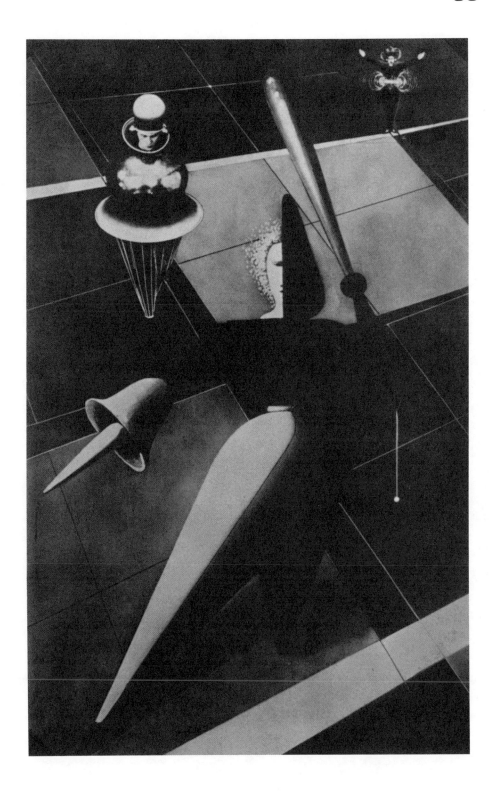

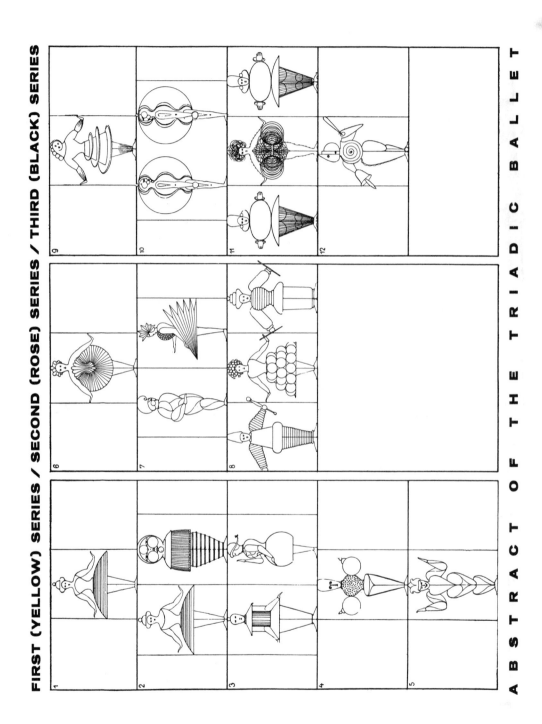

FIRST (YELLOW) SERIES / SECOND (ROSE) SERIES / THIRD (BLACK) SERIES

A B S T R A C T   O F   T H E   T R I A D I C   B A L L E T

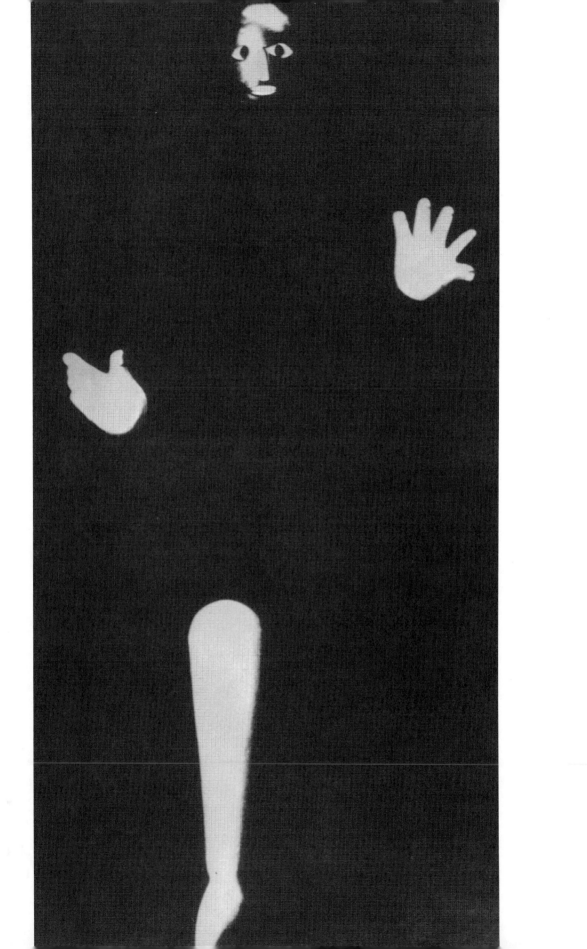

THE FIGURAL CABINET I. (First performance spring, 1922; second performance during the Bauhaus Week, 1923. Technical execution, Carl Schlemmer.)

"Half shooting gallery — half *metaphysicum abstractum*. Medley, i.e., variety of sense and nonsense, methodized by Color, Form, Nature, and Art; Man and Machine, Acoustics and Mechanics. Organization is everything; the most heterogeneous is the hardest to organize.

"The great green face, all nose, languishes for its vis-à-vis, where

woman peeks out, name's Gret,

she's got a blabbermouth and a swivelhead

and a nose like a trumpet!

Meta is physically complete: head and body disappear alternately.

The rainbow eye lights up.

"Slowly the figures march by: the white, yellow, red, blue ball walks; ball becomes pendulum; pendulum swings; clock runs. The Body-like-a-Violin, the Guy in Bright Checks, the Elemental One, the 'Better-Class Gent,' the Questionable One, Miss Rosy-Red, the Turk. The bodies look for heads, which are moving in opposite direction across the stage. A jerk, a bang, a victory march, whenever there is a union of head and body: the Hydrocephalus, the Body of Mary and the Body of the Turk, Diagonals, and the Body of the 'Better Gent.'

"Gigantic Hand says: Stop! — The varnished Angel ascends and twitters tru-lu-lu. . . .

"In the midst, the Master, E. T. A. Hoffmann's Spalanzani, spooking around, directing, gesticulating, telephoning, shooting himself in the head, and dying a thousand deaths from worry about the function of the functional.

"Imperturbably the window-shade roller unwinds, showing colored squares, an arrow and other signs, comma, parts of the body, numbers, advertisements: 'Open a Commercial Account,' 'Kukirol,' . . . At each side abstract linear figures with brass knobs and nickel bodies, their moods indicated by barometers.

"Bengal illumination. Fips the Terrier sits up. . . .

"The bell jangles. The Gigantic Hand — Green Man — Meta — The Bodies — . . . Barometers get out of hand; screw screws; an eye glows electrically; deafening sounds; Red. To end it all, the Master shoots himself — as the curtain falls — and this time successfully."

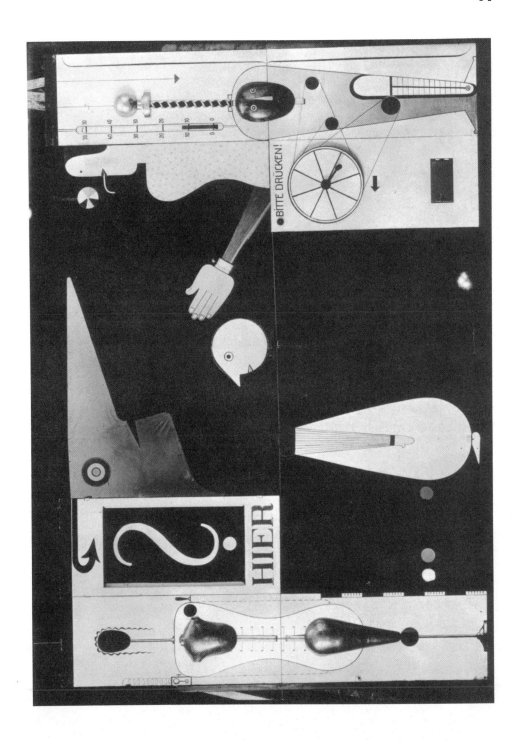

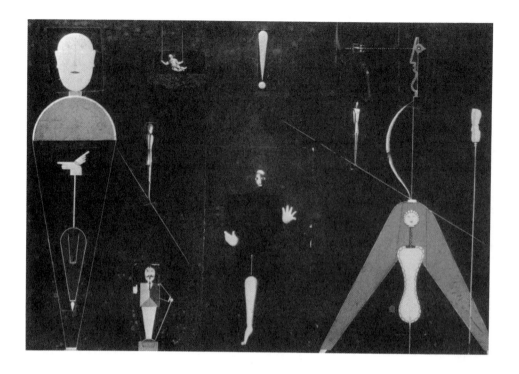

THE FIGURAL CABINET II. (Projected variation of previous.)
The Master of the previous performance is a dancing demon here (figure in center; also page 39). Metallic figures whiz and dash on wires from background to foreground and back again. Others float, soar, rotate, whir, rattle, speak, or sing.

SET for "Meta or the Pantomime of Places." Improvisation by the Bauhaus Stage. (First production Weimar, 1924.)

The various stages of a simple plot are freed from all accessories and paraphernalia; and the progression of the action is determined on the stage by means of placards such as: "Enter," "Exit," "Intermission," "Suspense," "1st, 2nd, 3rd Crisis," "Passion," "Conflict," "Climax," etc. — or, if necessary, it is announced from a portable scaffold. The actors perform the designated action at the appropriate spot. The props are: sofa, staircase, ladder, door, railing, horizontal bar.

SET for Hindemith-Kokoschka *Mörder Hoffnung der Frauen* (*Murderer, Hope of Women*). (Produced at Stuttgart Landestheater, 1921.)

By means of movable architectural props the prison tower is transformed into a gate of freedom. Form: musical architecture. Color: gloomy and ponderous, deep bronzes, black, light gray, English red. The Man is in nickel-plated armor; the Woman in a copper-colored gown.

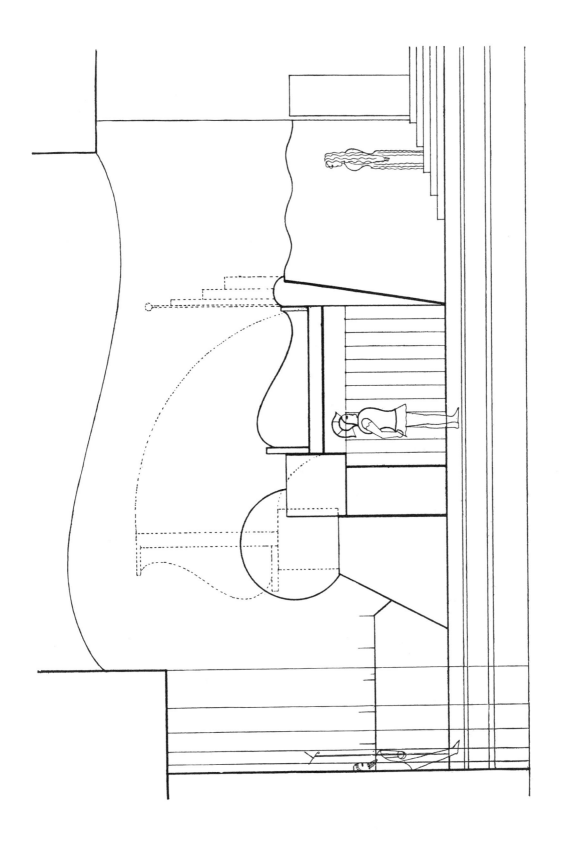

OSKAR SCHLEMMER   **Variations on a mask.**   Drawings for a class in stage theory.

OSKAR SCHLEMMER   **Costume designs for The Triadic Ballet.**

L. MOHOLY-NAGY

THEATER, CIRCUS, VARIETY

L. MOHOLY-NAGY
THEATER, CIRCUS, VARIETY

1. THE HISTORICAL THEATER

The historical theater was essentially a disseminator of information or propaganda, or it was an articulated concentration of action (*Aktionskonzentration*) derived from events and doctrines in their broadest meaning — that is to say, as "dramatized" legend, as religious (cultist) or political (proselytizing) propaganda, or as compressed action with a more or less transparent purpose behind it.

The theater differed from the eyewitness report, simple storytelling, didactic moralizing, or advertising copy through its own particular synthesis of the elements of presentation: SOUND, COLOR (LIGHT), MOTION, SPACE, FORM (OBJECTS AND PERSONS).

With these elements, in their accentuated but often uncontrolled interrelationships, the theater attempted to transmit an articulated experience.

In early epic drama (*Erzählungsdrama*) these elements were generally employed as illustration, subordinated to narration or propaganda. The next step in this evolution led to the drama of action (*Aktionsdrama*), where the elements of dynamic-dramatic movement began to crystallize: the theater of improvisation, the *commedia dell' arte*. These dramatic forms were progressively liberated from a central theme of logical, intellectual-emotional action which was no longer dominant. Gradually their moralizing and their

tendentiousness disappeared in favor of an unhampered concentration on action: Shakespeare, the opera.

With August Stramm, drama developed away from verbal context, from propaganda, and from character delineation, and toward explosive activism.[1] Creative experiments with MOTION AND SOUND (speech) were made, based on the impetus of human sources of energy, that is, the "passions." Stramm's theater did not offer narrative material, but action and tempo, which, unpremeditated, sprang almost AUTOMATICALLY and in headlong succession from the human impulse for motion. But even in Stramm's case action was not altogether free from literary encumbrance.

"Literary encumbrance" is the result of the unjustifiable transfer of intellectualized material from the proper realm of literary effectiveness (novel, short story, etc.) to the stage, where it incorrectly remains a dramatic end in itself. The result is nothing more than literature if a reality or a potential reality, no matter how imaginative, is formulated or visually expressed without the creative forms peculiar only to the stage. It is not until the tensions concealed in the utmost economy of means are brought into universal and dynamic interaction that we have creative stagecraft (*Bühnengestaltung*).[2] Even in recent times we have been deluded about the true value of creative stagecraft when revolutionary, social, ethical, or similar problems were unrolled with a great display of literary pomp and paraphernalia.

[1] August Stramm (1874–1915) was a Westphalian poet and dramatist and the strongest of the members of the circle known as the *Sturmdichter*. His works belong to the early phase of Expressionism and are in a radically elliptical, powerful, and antisyntactical style. His plays, *Sancta Susanna, Kräfte* (*Powers*, set to music in 1922 by Hindemith), *Erwachen* (*Awakening*), *Geschehen* (*Happening*), seem today less effective than his volumes of poetry, *Du* (*You*), *Tropfblut* (*Dripblood*). (Translator)

[2] *Gestaltung* was among the most fundamental terms in the language of the Bauhaus and is used many times by Schlemmer and Moholy in their writing, both by itself and in its many compounds, such as *Bühnengestaltung, Farbengestaltung, Theatergestaltung*. T. Lux Feininger writes: "If the term 'Bauhaus' was a new adaptation of the medieval concept of the 'Bauhütte,' the headquarters of the cathedral builders, the term 'Gestaltung' is old, meaningful and so nearly untranslatable that it has found its way into English usage. Beyond the significance of shaping, forming, thinking through, it has the flavor underlining the totality of such fashioning, whether of an artifact or of an idea. It forbids the nebulous and the diffuse. In its fullest philosophical meaning it expresses the Platonic *eidolon,* the *Urbild,* the pre-existing form." (Translator)

L. MOHOLY-NAGY   **The Benevolent Gentlemen (Circus Scene)**

2. ATTEMPTS AT A THEATER FORM FOR TODAY

a) Theater of Surprises: Futurists, Dadaists, Merz[3]

In the investigation of any morphology, we proceed today from the all-inclusive functionalism of goal, purpose, and materials.

From this premise the FUTURISTS, EXPRESSIONISTS, and DADAISTS (MERZ) came to the conclusion that phonetic word relationships were more significant than other creative literary means, and that the logical-intellectual content (*das Logisch-Gedankliche*) of a work of literature was far from its primary aim. It was maintained that, just as in representational painting it was not the content as such, not the objects represented which were essential, but the interaction of colors, so in literature it was not the logical-intellectual content which belonged in the foreground, but the effects which arose from the word-sound relationships. In the case of some writers this idea has been extended (or possibly contracted) to the point where word relationships are transformed into exclusively phonetic sound relationships, thereby totally fragmenting the word into conceptually disjointed vowels and consonants.

This was the origin of the Dadaist and Futurist "Theater of Surprises," a theater which aimed at the elimination of logical-intellectual (literary) aspects. Yet in spite of this, man, who until then had been the sole representative of logical, causal action and of vital mental activities, still dominated.

b) The Mechanized Eccentric (*Die mechanische Exzentrik*)

As a logical consequence of this there arose the need for a MECHANIZED ECCENTRIC, a concentration of stage action in its purest form (*eine Aktionskonzentration der Bühne in Reinkultur*). Man, who no longer should be permitted to represent himself as a phenomenon of spirit and mind through his intellectual and spiritual capacities, no longer has any place in this concentration of action. For, no matter how cultured he may be, his organism

---

[3] The phenomenon known as *Merz* is closely connected with the Dadaist movement of the post–World War I period in Germany and Switzerland. The term was coined in 1919 by the artist Kurt Schwitters and came from one of his collages in which was incorporated a scrap of newspaper with only the center part of the word "kom*merz*iell" on it. A whole series of his collages was called *Merzbilder*. From 1923 to 1932, with Arp, Lissitzsky, Mondrian, and many others, Schwitters published the magazine *Merz;* and at about the same period the Merz Poets caused a great furor. The movement was characterized by playfulness, earnest experimentalism, and what seems to have been a great need for self-expression and for shocking the bourgeoisie. (Translator)

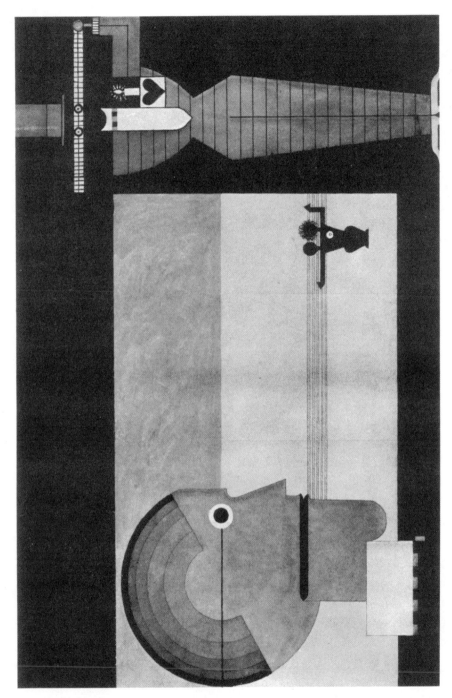

MARCEL BREUER

KURT SCHMIDT   **Stage Construction for the "Mechanical Ballet"**

permits him at best only a certain range of action, dependent entirely on his natural body mechanism.

The effect of this body mechanism (*Körpermechanik*) (in circus performance and athletic events, for example) arises essentially from the spectator's astonishment or shock at the potentialities of his *own* organism as demonstrated to him by others. This is a subjective effect. Here the human body is the sole medium of configuration (*Gestaltung*). For the purposes of an objective *Gestaltung* of movement this medium is limited, the more so since it has constant reference to sensible and perceptive (i.e., again literary) elements. The inadequacy of "human" *Exzentrik* led to the demand for a precise and fully controlled organization of form and motion, intended to be a synthesis of dynamically contrasting phenomena (space, form, motion, sound, and light). This is the Mechanized Eccentric. (See page 48.)

3. THE COMING THEATER: THEATER OF TOTALITY

Every form process or *Gestaltung* has its general as well as its particular

KURT SCHMIDT with F. W. BOGLER and GEORG TELTSCHER
The "Mechanical Ballet"   **Figurines A, B, and C**

KURT SCHMIDT with F. W. BOGLER and GEORG TELTSCHER
The "Mechanical Ballet"   **Figurines D and E**

The "Mechanical Ballet" was first performed at the Stadttheater in Jena during the Bauhaus Week (August, 1923).

KURT SCHMIDT   **Man + Machine**

premises, from which it must proceed in making use of its specific media. We might, therefore, clarify theater production (*Theatergestaltung*) if we investigated the nature of its highly controversial media: the human *word* and the human action, and, at the same time, considered the endless possibilities open to their creator — man.

The origins of MUSIC as conscious composition can be traced back to the melodic recitations of the heroic saga. When music was systematized, permitting only the use of HARMONIES (KLÄNGE) and excluding so-called SOUNDS (GERÄUSCHE), the only place left for a special sound form (*Geräuschgestaltung*) was in literature, particularly in poetry. This was the underlying idea from which the Expressionists, Futurists, and Dadaists proceeded in composing their sound-poems (*Lautgedichte*). But today, when music has been broadened to admit sounds of all kinds, the sensory-mechanistic effect of sound interrelationships is no longer a monopoly of poetry. It belongs, as much as do harmonies (*Töne*), to the realm of music, much in the same way that the task of painting, seen as color creation, is to organize clearly primary (apperceptive)[4] color effect. Thus the error of the Futurists, the Expressionists, the Dadaists, and all those who built on such foundations becomes clear. As an example: the idea of an *Exzentrik* which is ONLY mechanical.

It must be said, however, that those ideas, in contradistinction to a literary-illustrative viewpoint, have unquestionably advanced creative theater precisely because they were diametrically opposed. They canceled out the predominance of the exclusively logical-intellectual values. But once the predominance has been broken, the associative processes and the language of man, and consequently man himself in his totality as a formative medium for the stage, may not be barred from it. To be sure, he is no longer to be pivotal — as he is in traditional theater — but is to be employed ON AN EQUAL FOOTING WITH THE OTHER FORMATIVE MEDIA.

Man as the most active phenomenon of life is indisputably one of the most effective elements of a dynamic stage production (*Bühnengestaltung*), and therefore he justifies on functional grounds the utilization of his totality of action, speech, and thought. With his intellect, his dialectic, his adaptability to any situation by virtue of his control over his physical and mental powers, he is — when used in any concentration of action (*Aktionskonzentration*) — destined to be primarily a configuration of these powers.

And if the stage didn't provide him full play for these potentialities, it would be imperative to create an adequate vehicle.

But this utilization of man must be clearly differentiated from his appearance heretofore in traditional theater. While there he was only the interpreter

---

[4] "Apperceptive" signifies here, in contrast to "associative," an elementary step in observation and conceptualization (psychophysical assimilation). E.g., to assimilate a color = apperceptive process. The human eye reacts without previous experience to red with green, blue with yellow, etc. An object = assimilation of color + matter + form = connection with previous experience = associative process.

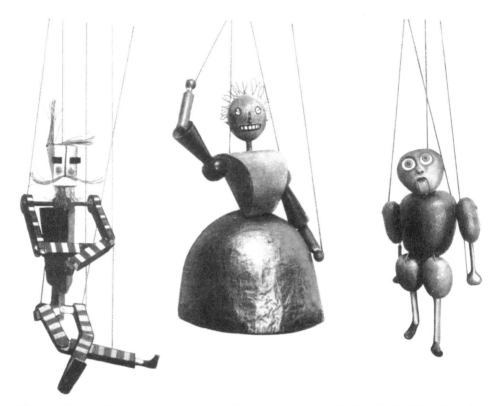

**Figures from the marionette play *The Adventures of the Little Hunchback.*
The Tailor; his Wife; the Hunchback.**
Design: KURT SCHMIDT. Execution: T. HERGT

of a literarily conceived individual or type, in the new THEATER OF TOTALITY he will use the spiritual and physical means at his disposal PRODUCTIVELY and from his own INITIATIVE submit to the over-all action process.

While during the Middle Ages (and even today) the center of gravity in theater production lay in the representation of the various *types* (hero, harlequin, peasant, etc.), it is the task of the FUTURE ACTOR to discover and activate that which is COMMON to all men.

In the plan of such a theater the traditionally "meaningful" and causal inter-connections can NOT play the major role. In the consideration of stage setting as an *art form*, we must learn from the creative artist that, just as it is im-possible to ask what a man (as organism) is or stands for, it is inadmissible

Figures from the marionette play *The Adventures of the Little Hunchback*.
The Hunchback; the Hangman; the Ointment Merchant.
Design: KURT SCHMIDT. Execution: T. HERGT

to ask the same question of a contemporary nonobjective picture which likewise is a *Gestaltung*, that is, an organism.

The contemporary painting exhibits a multiplicity of color and surface interrelationships, which gain their effect, on the one hand, from their conscious and logical statement of problems, and on the other, from the unanalyzable intangibles of creative intuition.

In the same way, the Theater of Totality with its multifarious complexities of light, space, plane, form, motion, sound, man — and with all the possibilities for varying and combining these elements — must be an ORGANISM.

Thus the process of integrating man into creative stage production must be unhampered by moralistic tendentiousness or by problems of science or the INDIVIDUAL. Man may be active only as the bearer of those functional elements which are organically in accordance with his specific nature.

It is self-evident, however, that all *other* means of stage production must be given positions of effectiveness equal to man's, who as a living psychophysical organism, as the producer of incomparable climaxes and infinite variations, demands of the coformative factors a high standard of quality.

4. HOW SHALL THE THEATER OF TOTALITY BE REALIZED?

One of two points of view still important today holds that theater is the concentrated activation (*Aktionskonzentration*) of sound, light (color), space, form, and motion. Here man as coactor is not necessary, since in our day equipment can be constructed which is far more capable of executing the *purely mechanical* role of man than man himself.

The other, more popular view will not relinquish the magnificent instrument which is man, even though no one has yet solved the problem of how to employ him as a creative medium on the stage.

Is it possible to include his human, logical functions in a present-day concentration of action on the stage, without running the risk of producing a copy from nature and without falling prey to Dadaist or Merz characterization, composed of an eclectic patchwork whose seeming order is purely arbitrary?

The creative arts have discovered pure media for their constructions: the primary relationships of color, mass, material, etc. But how can we integrate a sequence of human movements and thoughts on an equal footing with the controlled, "absolute" elements of sound, light (color), form, and motion? In this regard only summary suggestions can be made to the creator of the new theater (*Theatergestalter*). For example, the REPETITION of a thought by many actors, with identical words and with identical or varying intonation and cadence, could be employed as a means of creating synthetic (i.e., unifying) creative theater. (This would be the CHORUS — but not the attendant and passive chorus of antiquity!) Or mirrors and optical equipment could be used to project the gigantically enlarged faces and gestures of the actors, while their voices could be amplified to correspond with the visual MAGNIFICATION. Similar effects can be obtained from the SIMULTANE-OUS, SYNOPTICAL, and SYNACOUSTICAL reproduction of thought (with motion pictures, phonographs, loud-speakers), or from the reproduction of thoughts suggested by a construction of variously MESHING GEARS (*eine* ZAHNRADARTIG INEINANDERGREIFENDE *Gedankengestaltung*).

Independent of work in music and acoustics, the literature of the future will create its own "harmonies," at first primarily adapted to its own media, but with far-reaching implications for others. These will surely exercise an influence on the word and thought constructions of the stage.

This means, among other things, that the phenomena of the subconscious and dreams of fantasy and reality, which up to now were central to the so-called "INTIMATE ART THEATER" ("KAMMERSPIELE"), may no longer be predominant. And even if the conflicts arising from today's complicated social patterns, from the world-wide organization of technology, from pacifist-utopian and other kinds of revolutionary movements, can have a place in the art of the stage, they will be significant only in a transitional period, since their treatment belongs properly to the realms of literature, politics, and philosophy.

We envision TOTAL STAGE ACTION (GESAMTBÜHNENAKTION) as a great dynamic-rhythmic process, which can compress the greatest clashing masses

or accumulations of media — as qualitative and quantitative tensions — into elemental form. Part of this would be the use of simultaneously inter-penetrating sets of contrasting relationships, which are of minor importance in themselves, such as: the tragicomic, the grotesque-serious, the trivial-monumental; hydraulic spectacles; acoustical and other "pranks"; and so on. Today's CIRCUS, OPERETTA, VAUDEVILLE, the CLOWNS in America and elsewhere (Chaplin, Fratellini) have accomplished great things, both in this respect and in eliminating the subjective — even if the process has been naïve and often more superficial than incisive. Yet it would be just as superficial if we were to dismiss great performances and "shows" in this genre with the word *Kitsch*. (See pages 51, 65, 69.) It is high time to state once and for all that the much disdained masses, despite their "academic backwardness," often exhibit the soundest instincts and preferences. Our task will always remain the creative understanding of the true, and not the imagined, needs.

5. THE MEANS

Every *Gestaltung* or creative work should be an unexpected and new organism, and it is natural and incumbent on us to draw the material for surprise effects from our daily living. Nothing is more effective than the exciting new possibilities offered by the familiar and yet not properly evaluated elements of modern life — that is, its idiosyncrasies: individuation, classification, mechanization. With this in mind, it is possible to arrive at a proper understanding of stagecraft through an investigation of creative media other than man-as-actor himself.

In the future, SOUND EFFECTS will make use of various acoustical equipment driven electrically or by some other mechanical means. Sound waves issuing from unexpected sources — for example, a speaking or singing arc lamp, loud-speakers under the seats or beneath the floor of the auditorium, the use of new amplifying systems — will raise the audience's acoustic surprise-threshold so much that unequal effects in other areas will be disappointing.

COLOR (LIGHT) must undergo even greater transformation in this respect than sound.

L. MOHOLY-NAGY   **Human Mechanics (Variety)**

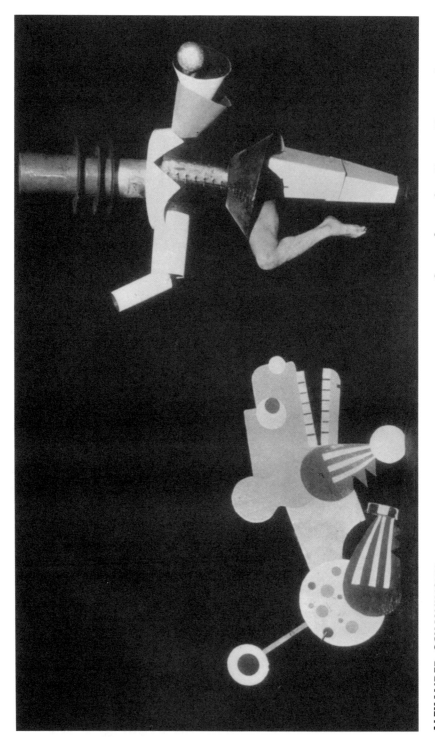

ALEXANDER SCHAWINSKY

Scene from the Circus. First performance
1924 at the Bauhaus.

Developments in painting during the past decades have created the organization of absolute color values and, as a consequence, the supremacy of pure and luminous chromatic tones. Naturally the monumentality and the lucid balance of their harmonies will not tolerate the actor with indistinct or splotchy make-up and tattered costuming, a product of misunderstood Cubism, Futurism, etc. The use of precision-made metallic masks and costumes and those of various other composition materials will thus become a matter of course. The pallid face, the subjectivity of expression, and the gestures of the actor in a colored stage environment are therefore eliminated without impairing the effective contrast between the human body and any mechanical construction. Films can also be projected onto various surfaces and further experiments in space illumination will be devised. This will constitute the new ACTION OF LIGHT, which by means of modern technology will use the most intensified contrasts to guarantee itself a position of importance equal to that of all other theater media. We have not yet begun to realize the potential of light for sudden or blinding illumination, for flare effects, for phosphorescent effects, for bathing the auditorium in light synchronized with climaxes or with the total extinguishing of lights on the stage. All this, of course, is thought of in a sense totally different from anything in current traditional theater.

From the time that stage objects became mechanically movable, the generally traditional, horizontally structured organization of movement in space has been enriched by the possibility of vertical motion. Nothing stands in the way of making use of complex APPARATUS such as film, automobile, elevator, airplane, and other machinery, as well as optical instruments, reflecting equipment, and so on. The current demand for dynamic construction will be satisfied in this way, even though it is still only in its first stages.

There would be a further enrichment if the present isolation of the stage could be eliminated. In today's theater, STAGE AND SPECTATOR are too much separated, too obviously divided into active and passive, to be able to produce creative relationships and reciprocal tensions.

It is time to produce a kind of stage activity which will no longer permit the masses to be silent spectators, which will not only excite them inwardly but will let them *take hold and participate* — actually allow them to fuse with the action on the stage at the peak of cathartic ecstasy.

To see that such a process is not chaotic, but that it develops with control and organization, will be one of the tasks of the thousand-eyed NEW DIRECTOR, equipped with all the modern means of understanding and communication.

It is clear that the present peep-show stage is not suitable for such organized motion.

The next form of the advancing theater — in cooperation with future authors — will probably answer the above demands with SUSPENDED BRIDGES AND DRAWBRIDGES running horizontally, diagonally, and vertically within the space of the theater; with platform stages built far into the auditorium; and so on. Apart from rotating sections, the stage will have movable space constructions and DISKLIKE AREAS, in order to bring certain action moments on the stage into prominence, as in film "close-ups." In place of today's periphery of orchestra loges, a runway joined to the stage could be built to establish — by means of a more or less caliperlike embrace — a closer connection with the audience.

The possibilities for a VARIATION OF LEVELS OF MOVABLE PLANES on the stage of the future would contribute to a genuine organization of space. Space will then no longer consist of the interconnections of planes in the old meaning, which was able to conceive of architectonic delineation of space only as an enclosure formed by opaque surfaces. The new space originates from free-standing surfaces or from linear definition of planes (WIRE FRAMES, ANTENNAS), so that the surfaces stand at times in a very free relationship to one another, without the need of any direct contact. (See page 69.)

As soon as an intense and penetrating concentration of action can be functionally realized, there will develop simultaneously the corresponding auditorium ARCHITECTURE. There will also appear COSTUMES designed to

L. MOHOLY-NAGY

**Stage Scene
Loud-speaker**

emphasize function and costumes which are conceived only for single moments of action and capable of sudden transformations.

There will arise an enhanced *control* over all formative media, unified in a harmonious effect and built into an organism of perfect equilibrium.

Bauhaus stage class.

FARKAS MOLNÁR
U-THEATER

FARKAS MOLNÁR   **U-Theater in action.**

4

FARKAS MOLNÁR

U-THEATER

1. THE DIVISION OF THE STAGE

A. First stage

A square area ca. 36 x 36 feet which can be raised and lowered as a whole or in separate sections. For spatial productions such as human and mechanical performances, dance, acrobatics, vaudeville (experimental work; *Exzentrik*), etc. Action on the stage proper is visible from three sides, i.e., up to 270 degrees, depending on the requirements of any given action.

B. Second stage

A platform ca. 18 x 36 feet which slides forward or backward at the height of the front row of seats in the auditorium; it can also be raised or lowered. This stage is for three-dimensional scenery, which, however, does not need to be seen fully in the round. Sets can be prepared behind the curtain, invisible to the audience, and then rolled out on this Stage B. The curtain consists of two metal sheets which can be pulled laterally into the "wings."

C. Third stage

A stage surface enclosed at the rear and at the sides, open to the audience (the largest proscenium opening is 36 x 24 feet). The platform itself can be moved to the rear or to either side (1, 2, 3, 4, 5), so that here as well preparations can be made out of sight. To be used for painted flats which need to be handled from behind, from the sides, and from above. This stage can be used also for traditional intimate theater productions (*Kammerspiele*).

Any of the three stages can be used for an orchestra, depending on where the sound is to come from — or on which stage is not being used for the action. Of the three stages, Stage A has the greatest and most intimate contact with the audience; for this reason its forward areas are best for action demanding this contact. The combined Stage A–B also lends itself well to real audience participation.

2. SUBSIDIARY PARTS OF THE STAGE

D. Fourth stage

A suspended stage above Stage B, equipped with a sounding board. It is connected with the first balcony. For both music and stage action.

E. Elevator and lighting apparatus

A cylindrical construction movable in all directions above Stage A–B and above the auditorium; used to lower people and equipment. Attached to the underside of the cylinder is a bridge by means of which the balconies can be reached. This serves the double purpose of having built-in spotlights and illuminating fixtures, and of making aerial acrobatics possible.

F.

Mechanical music apparatus, combinations of modern sound-effects instruments, radio, and lighting effects.

G.

Suspended bridges, drawbridges between the stages and balconies. Other mechanical aids for the heightening of various effects, hydraulic apparatus (for fountains, etc.), machines for dispersing odors of various kinds.

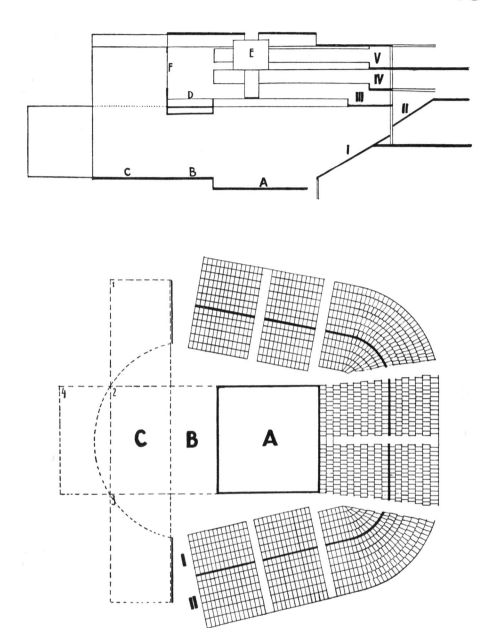

FARKAS MOLNÁR   **The U-Theater in Action**

3. THE AUDITORIUM

I and II

Two U-shaped rings, built in the form of an amphitheater. Adjustable and rotating seats provide the best possible view of any action in the theater. Numerous connecting aisles and other means of access to the stage. A space between the first and second rings; the second ring higher than the first. I and II together seat 1200 persons.

III

A single balcony, connected with the suspended stage (D); its two rows together seat 150 persons.

IV and V

Two rows of loges, one above the other; each box seats 6 persons. Total: 240 seats. The dividing walls are removable or can be variously rearranged.

Public rooms, entrances, vestibule, stairways, checkrooms, restaurants, and bars lie outside the confines of the present sketch, and are still in the planning stage.

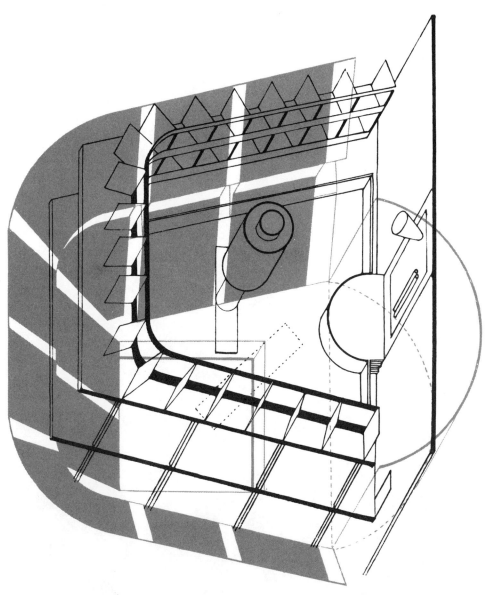

FARKAS MOLNÁR

U-Theater

The Building as Stage.

Photograph: Lux Feininger.

The modern building with its series of traversable roof areas, terraces, and verandas will make the ideal outdoor stage of the future.

OSKAR SCHLEMMER
THEATER (BÜHNE)

5

OSKAR SCHLEMMER
THEATER (BÜHNE)

From a lecture-demonstration at the Bauhaus by Oskar Schlemmer to The Circle of Friends of the Bauhaus, March 16, 1927.

Before speaking about theater proper at the Bauhaus, we should first take a brief look at the way in which it came about, consider the justification for its existence, and observe its path and its goals. In short, we should review its primary endeavor, which is to approach all our material from a basic and elementary standpoint. It is because of this endeavor that the stage here has became an organic link in the total chain of Bauhaus activity.

It is natural that the aims of the Bauhaus — to seek the union of the artistic-ideal with the craftsmanlike-practical by thoroughly investigating the creative elements, and to understand in all its ramifications the essence of *der Bau,* creative construction — have valid application to the field of the theater. For, like the concept of *Bau* itself, the stage is an orchestral complex which comes about only through the cooperation of many different forces. It is the union of the most heterogeneous assortment of creative elements. Not the least of its functions is to serve the metaphysical needs of man by constructing a world of illusion and by creating the transcendental on the basis of the rational.

The Auditorium (Aula)
Nickel-plated steel-frame chairs with canvas seats: Marcel Breuer.
Ceiling lights: Krajewski.   Photograph: Consemüller.

From the first day of its existence, the Bauhaus sensed the impulse for creative theater; for from that first day the play instinct (*der Spieltrieb*) was present. The play instinct, which Schiller in his wonderful and enduring *Briefe über die ästhetische Erziehung des Menschen* (*Letters on the Aesthetic Education of Man*, 1795) calls the source of man's real creative values, is the un-self-conscious and naïve pleasure in shaping and producing, without asking questions about use or uselessness, sense or nonsense, good or bad. This pleasure through creation was especially strong at the beginning (not to say the infancy) of the Bauhaus

in Weimar

and was expressed in our exuberant parties, in improvisations, and in the imaginative masks and costumes which we made.

We might say that during the course of its development, this state of naïveté, which is the womb of the play instinct, is generally followed by a period of reflection, doubt, and criticism, something that in turn can easily bring about the destruction of the original state, unless a second and, as it were, skeptical kind of naïveté tempers this critical phase. Today we have become much more aware of ourselves. A sense for standards and constants has arisen out of the unconscious and the chaotic. This, together with concepts such as norm, type, and synthesis, points the way to creative form (*Gestaltung*).[1]

It was due only to intense skepticism, for example, that in 1922 Lothar Schreyer's plan to form a Bauhaus theater failed; at the time there was practically no climate for strong philosophical points of view (*Weltanschauungstendenzen*), none at least which could be found in the sacral garb of Expressionism. On the other hand, there was a distinct feeling for satire and parody. It was probably a legacy of the Dadaists to ridicule automatically everything that smacked of solemnity or ethical precepts. And so the grotesque flourished again. It found its nourishment in travesty and in mocking the antiquated forms of the contemporary theater. Though its tendency was fundamentally negative, its evident recognition of the origin, conditions, and laws of theatrical play was a positive feature.

[1] For a discussion of the significance of the word *Gestaltung* in the language of the Bauhaus, see note 2, page 50. (Translator)

The Stage / with openings toward both the main hall (Aula) and the canteen / Technical equipment: Joost Schmidt / Lighting: A. E. G. — Berlin.

Photograph: Consemüller.

The 72 square meters of skeletal platform components permit a 50–centimeter raising of the entire stage floor or can serve as sectional set props. On the ceiling, a four-row track system for movable walls, suspended props, and so on.
Architect: Walter Gropius.

The dance, however, stayed alive throughout this period. During the course of our growth it changed from the crude country dancing of our "youth hostelers" (*Rüpeltanz der Wandervögel*) to the full-dress fox trot. The same thing happened in music: our concertina metamorphosed into our jazz band (A. Weininger). Group dancing found its image reflected on the stage in the dance of the individual. And from this developed our formalized use of color (*das Farbig-Formale*), and the Mechanical Ballet (K. Schmidt, Bogler, Teltscher). Experimentation with colored light and shadows became the "Reflectory Light Play" (Schwertfeger and L. Hirschfeld-Mack). A marionette theater was begun.

While we had no stage of our own in Weimar and had to give our productions on a sort of dubious suburban podium there, since the move

Model for a Mechanical Stage by Heinz Loew.

The illustration shows the basic elements of a mechanical stage with a three-track system (a, b, c) and two rotary disks (d) which put in motion

a) rectilinear-static

b) eccentric-dynamic

c) translucent-surface   } elements

d) stabile three-dimensional

The interaction of the various movable objects is controlled mechanically and can be varied in accordance with the desired composition.

A word in general about stage mechanics:

In compliance with a curious and misleading "instinct," there is a feeling today that every technical stage effect should be scrupulously hidden from audience view. Paradoxically, this often results in backstage activities becoming the more interesting aspect of the theater. This is especially true in this age of technology and the machine. — Most stages possess a vast technical apparatus, representing a great deal of energy and work, of which, however, the audience has hardly an inkling. It would seem that a task for the future would be to develop a technical personnel as important as the actors, one whose job it would be to bring this apparatus into view in its peculiar and novel beauty, undisguised and as an end in itself.   H. L.

to Dessau

we have been in the enviable position of having a "house-stage" of our own in the new Bauhaus building. Although it was originally meant to be a platform for lectures as well as a stage for performances on a limited scale, it is nevertheless well equipped for a serious approach to stage problems.

For us these problems and their solution lie in fundamentals, in elementary matters, in discovering literally the primary meaning of Stage. We are concerned with what makes things typical, with type, with number and measure, with basic law. ● ● ● I scarcely need to say that these concerns have been active, if not necessarily dominant, during all periods of great art; but they could be active only when preconditioned by a state of hypersensitive alertness and tension, that is, when functioning as the regulators of a real feeling of involvement with the world and life. Of many memorable statements which have been made about number, measure, and law in art, I cite only one sentence from Philipp Otto Runge: "It is precisely in the case of those works of art which most truly arise from the imagination and the mystique of our soul, unhampered by externals and unburdened by history, that the strictest regularity is necessary."[2]

If the aims of the Bauhaus are also the aims of our stage, it is natural that the following elements should be of first and foremost importance to us: SPACE as a part of the larger total complex, building (*Bau*). The art of the stage is a spatial art, a fact which is bound to become clearer and clearer in the future. The stage, including the auditorium, is above all an architectonic-spatial organism where all things happening to it and within it exist in a spatially conditioned relationship. ● ● An aspect of space is FORM, comprising both surface (that is, two-dimensional) form and plastic (three-dimensional) form. Aspects of form are COLOR and LIGHT, to which we attach a new importance. We are primarily visually oriented beings and can therefore take pleasure in the purely optical; we can manipulate forms and discover mysterious and surprising effects in mechanical motion from con-

---

2 Philipp Otto Runge (1777–1810) was the North German painter whose remarkable union of artistic theory and practice and whose intimate association with the Romantic poets make it easier to say of him than of any other individual that he was the real father of the Romantic School in German art. (See Fritz Novotny's chapter on Runge in his *Painting and Sculpture in Europe: 1780–1880*, Pelican History of Art series [Baltimore, Penguin Books, 1960], pp. 59–65.) (Translator)

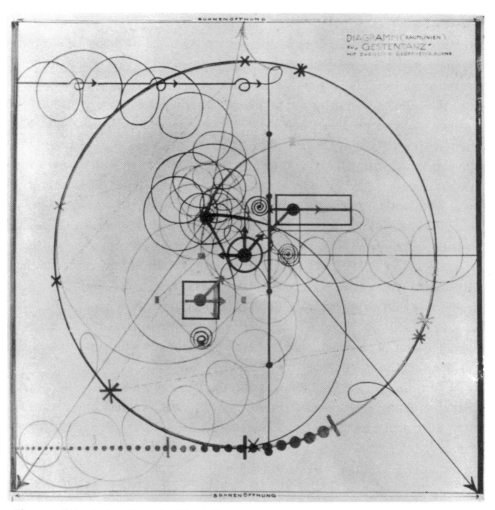

Diagram of the Gesture Dance by Oskar Schlemmer.

Photograph: Hatzold.

The diagram, giving a linear indication of the paths of motion and a projection of forward movement on the stage surface, is meant to be an aid in establishing graphically the total course of the action. A second kind of aid is to describe this action in words (see accompanying text). Each of these representational means complements the other. Yet, in spite of the directions for tempo and sound, they are incapable of giving an exhaustive picture of the performance. Still missing are precise indications of gesture (movements of torso, legs, arms, and hands), of mimetics (motions of the head, facial expression), of voice pitch, and so on. — Our point here is to suggest the difficulty of the problem of preparing a script for dance and other stage action. The more completely such a script tries to fix the total action, the more the multitude of essential details complicates the matter and obscures the very purpose of such a score, namely, legibility.

g e s t e n t a n z

geräusche **A** der gelbe **B** der rote **C** der blaue sek.

	von links vorn	
	spr ngt expressiv	
	5 schritte vor _____	3
	rasch rückwärts zurück _____	5
	in trippelschritt	
	7 schritte vor	5
	rasch rückwärts zurück _____	7
	9 schritte vor u n d _____	7
klavier:	in großen triumfierenden	*von links hinten*	
„a-u-f i-n d-e-n	marschschritten	**3 schritte vor** _____	3
k-a-m-p-f . . . ." vor **nickel**stuhl	rasch kehrt!	12
	1 schritt seite ●_____	**3 schritte vor** _____	1:3
	1 schritt rücken ●_____	rasch kehrt!	1:3
	1 schritt seite ●_____	3 schritte vor _____	1:3
	1 schritt vorn u n d _____	rasch kehrt!	1:3
	s i t z t ! ! ! ! ! ! ! ! !	**reckt sich hoch auf!**	1:3
	streckt bein ▬ _____	blickt scharf auf drehstuhl _____	1:3
	legt arm ▬	mitte	1:3
	wirft kopf!	scharf in gerader linie _____	1:3
		vor _____	7 2
		k e h r t !	1
		ebenso **zurück** _____	5
		k e h r t !	1
		ebenso **vor** _____	4
		k e h r t !	1
		zurück, dann _____	3
		vor stuhl, dann _____	2
		ü b e r stuhl . . . . *von mitte rechts* _____	1
		kreuzquer ✕ _____	kriecht langgestreckt	1
		kreuzquer ✕ _____	herein	1
		kreuzquer ✕ u n d _____	bis _____	1
		s i t z t ! ! ! ! ! ! ! ! !	vor bank _____	1
	schnellt hoch!!!!!!!!!!!!!! und schnellt sofort hoch!!! schnellt hoch!!!!!!!!!!!!!!	1
	s-e-t-z-e-n s-i-c-h z-e-i-t-l-u-p-e-n-h-a-f-t l-a-n-g-s-a-m⎫	8
eigenstimmen:	**b**SSSSSSSSSSSSSSSSSSSSSSSSSSSSSSSSSSSSSSSSSSSSSSSSSSSSSSSSSSSSSSSSS⎭	
gong!	**sitzt!** _____ **sitzt!** ▬▬ **sitzt!** ▬▬▬	1
	— —	8
	wendet sich zu **B**———→ *wendet sich zu* **A**———→ selbstversunken _____	1
	w i n s e l n falsettgespräch selig trunken _____	21
	wendet sich zu **C**———→	3
	vorgebeugt _____ v e r s t ä n d n i s i n n i g e s gemaunze	15
	sagt **B** *was ins ohr* ———→ *hält hand ans ohr* ←———	9
	a-r-m-s-c-h-w-u-n-g-g-e-l-ä-c-h-t-e-r selbstversunken _____	15
	hält hand ans ohr ←——— *sagt* **A** *was ins ohr* ———→ selig trunken	9
	v e r g n ü g l i c h e s h ä n d e r e i b e n _____	12
	hält hand ans ohr ———→ *sagt* **B** *was ins ohr* ←——— _____	9
	k ● ö ● r ● p ● e ● e ● r ● g ● e ● e ● l ● ä ● c ● h ● t ● e ● e ● r	15
fall	reckt sich scharf nach reckt sich scharf nach reckt sich kerzengerade	1
	vorn! hinten! hoch!	
uhr schlägt	1——2——3——4—½5——6——7——8——9—¾10——11—½12	42
	l-a-u-s-c-h-e-n a-n-g-e-s-p-a-n-n-t	
wecker rasselt	schnellen hoch und drehen sich wie besessen um sich selbst	21
dumpfe pauke	g-e-h-e-n l-a-n-g-s-a-m i-n t-a-p-p-s-c-h-r-i-t-t-e-n a-u-f	
	s-i-c-h z-u. je näher desto rollender und	
	u-n-t-e-r arm- und körper-bewegungen	
	d-i-c-h-t b-e-i-s-a-m-m-e-n s-i-c-h i-n s-i-c-h	
	v-e-r-m-a-s-s-e-l-n-d m-u-r-m-e-l-n-d:	
	l-a-m-i-r-u-s-o-l-a-m-i-r-u-s-o-l-a-m-i-r-u-s-o-l-a-m-i-r-u	30
schlag!!!!!!!!!!!!! s c h r e c k e n h o c h !!!!!!!!!!!!	1
p f i f f f ! rennt scharf nach ecke rennt scharf nach mitte rennt scharf nach ecke	
	links vorn hinten rechts vorn	5
	s t i e r e n s t a r r i n s l e e r e h i n a u s	12
	???	
dumpfe pauken-	i-n w-e-i-t-a-u-s-h-o-l-e-n-d-e-n t-e-i-g-s-c-h-r-i-t-t-e-n	
sch.äge *wie tropfen*	i-m k-r-e-i-s-e g-e-h-e-n-d _____	14
	schrecksprung! s t i e r e n a u f **A**	1:4
	s-t-a-p-f-e-n w-e-i-t-e-r t-e-i-g-s-c-h-r-i-t-t k-r-e-i-s	1?
	schrecksprung! (kürzer) s t i e r e n a u f **A**	1:4
	s-t-a-p-f-e-n w-e-i-t-e-r t-e-i-g-s-c-h-r-i-t-t	8
	schrecksprung! (kurz) s t i e r e n a u f **A**	1:4
stimme: brüder!	b i e g e n s c h a r f a b! bedeutend auf mitte	
	mit ausgestrecktem arm _____	3
	h a n d a u f l e g e n _____	9
fanfare! . . . . s c h w u r !	7
kitsch grammo-		
phon spielt:	♪ (Großmütterlein! Großmütterlein! usw.)	15
	rotieren sich wiegend im walzertakt zu ihren ausgängen hinaus	
—2—3—**4**	aus ausgangstür in ausfallstellung	4
paukenschläge	**rechtes bein vor!** ▬ **armkraftgeste** _____	3
-5-!	**rasch weg!** _____	1

cealed sources; we can convert and transfigure space through form, color, and light. ● ● We can say, therefore, that the concept *Schau-Spiel* would become a reality if all these elements, comprehended as a totality, were brought into being.[3] We should then have a real "feast for the eyes," a metaphor come true. ● ● ● If, going even beyond this, we atomize the constricting space of the stage and translate it into terms of the total building itself, the exterior as well as the interior — a thought which is particularly fascinating in view of the new Bauhaus building (illust. page 78) — then the idea of a *space stage* would be demonstrated in a way which is probably altogether unprecedented.

We can imagine plays whose "plots" consist of nothing more than the pure movement of forms, color, and light. If this movement is to be a mechanical process without human involvement of any sort (except for the man at the control panel), we shall have to have equipment similar to the precision machinery of the perfectly constructed automaton. ● ● Today's technology already has the necessary apparatus. It is a question of money — and, more importantly, a question as to how successfully such a technical expenditure can meet the desired effect. How long, that is, can any rotating, vibrating, whirring contrivance, together with an infinite variety of forms, colors, and lights, sustain the interest of the spectator? The question, in short, is whether the purely mechanical stage can be accepted as an independent genre, and whether, in the long run, it will be able to do without that being who would be acting here solely as the "perfect machinist" and inventor, namely, the *human* being.[4]

[3] *Schau-Spiel. Das Schauspiel*, the German word for play, drama, or spectacle, takes on its literal meaning of a "visual play" or a "show" in this hyphenated form. (Translator)

[4] To avoid ambiguity, it should be said that we are speaking here of a self-contained mechanical stage device, not of the mechanized and remodeled total stage organization, which will come with the building of the new theater of steel, concrete, and glass, and whose revolving stages, integrated film projection, and so forth, are all meant to function as foils for human activity on the stage. ● ● The Piscator Theater designed by Gropius is intended to provide for the realization of such plans. ● ● A utopian project not feasible at the present is seen in the Spherical Theater (*Kugeltheater*, page 89). (Author) [See Dr. Gropius' Introduction to this book; see also S. Giedion, *Walter Gropius: Work and Teamwork* (New York, Reinhold Publishing Corp., 1954), pp. 8, 50, 61–66, 151, 154–157, 240, 243; and James Marston Fitch, *Walter Gropius* (New York, George Braziller, Inc., 1960), pp. 21–23, and illustrations 54–61. (Translator)]

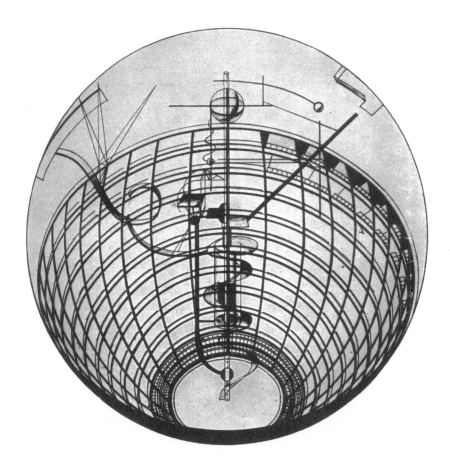

The Spherical Theater, designed by Andreas Weininger.

An answer to the question of the space theater, the problem of the theater of the future. — The space stage and the space theater as the home of the mechanical play. Motion: the point of departure for all primary media: space, body, line, point, color, light; sound, noise; in a new mechanical synthesis (as opposed to the static synthesis of architecture).

A sphere as architectonic structure in place of the customary theater. The spectators, on the inner wall of the sphere, find themselves in a new relationship to space. Because of their all-encompassing view, because of centripetal force, they find themselves in a new psychic, optical, acoustical relationship; they find themselves confronted with new possibilities for concentric, eccentric, multidirectional, mechanical space-stage phenomena. — In order to realize its task completely, the mechanical theater lays claim to the highest developments of functional technology. — Purpose: to educate men through the creative play of new rhythms of motion to new modes of observation; to give elementary answers to elementary necessities.   A. W.

ALFRED'S COLLEGE
LIBRARY

Since we do not yet have a perfected mechanical stage (the technical equipping of our own experimental stage lags for the time being far behind that of the government-subsidized stages), man remains perforce our essential element. And of course he will remain so as long as the stage exists. In contradistinction to the rationalistically determined world of space, form, and color, man is the vessel of the subconscious, the unmediated experience, and the transcendental. He is the organism of flesh and blood, conditioned by measure and by time. And he is the herald, indeed he is the creator, of possibly the most important element of theater: SOUND, WORD, LANGUAGE.

We confess that up to now we have cautiously avoided experimenting with this element of language, not in order to de-emphasize it but, conscious of its significance, to master it slowly. For the time being we must be content with the silent play of gesture and motion — that is, with *pantomime* — firmly believing that one day the *word* will develop automatically from it. Our decision to approach the human word "unliterarily," in its primary state, as a happening, as if it were being heard for the first time, makes this particular field a problem and a challenge.

> Since the above was written, we have learned from an experiment along these lines called "House π" that an approach to word development within the dramatic process as suggested above is a thoroughly tenable one. Starting with a prepared stage with its own set of spatial relationships (involving various levels constructed of movable skeletal boxes with flooring where needed), and with experimental light effects, it was possible to obtain through pure chance, inspiration, and the extemporizing of the participants an "extract," which, as it developed, became more fascinating, the clearer the possibility became of giving the action a definitive form. It was demonstrated here, too, that the growth of a scene must follow ultimately a rhythmical and somehow mathematically determinable law, perhaps most closely akin to the laws of music, without, however, its involving music as such.

What has been said about word and language applies also to SOUND and HARMONY. Here too we try in our own way to create out of necessity and need an appropriate aural expression for each experimental production (*Gestaltung*). For the time being, such simple "stimulators" as the gong and kettledrum are enough.

A brief word about our series of stage demonstrations:[5] First of all, when confronted with any new thing, we are accustomed to pause and investigate its essence. We generally do this with both skepticism and a kind of buoyancy. ● ● Let us begin with the curtain and investigate this object as a *Ding an sich*, with an eye to its essential and to its particular properties. ● ● Together with the ramp, it separates the two worlds of auditorium and stage into two hostile-friendly camps. It imposes a state of excitement on both sides. Out there the audience's excitement asks: What's going to happen? Back here our question is: What's going to be the effect? ● ● "The curtain goes up!" ● ● But how? It can go up in any of a hundred different ways. Whether in the matter-of-fact tempo of "now-it's-open, now-it's-closed," or solemnly and sedately rising, or torn open with two or three violent tugs, the curtain has its special vocabulary. We can imagine a curtain-play which would evolve literally from its own "material" and reveal in an entertaining way the curtain's own secret nature. ● ● ● By adding an actor, the possibilities of this sort of play are further multiplied.

Let us now take a look at the empty stage and by means of linear division organize it in such a way as to be able to understand its space. We first divide the square surface of the floor in the middle and then into bisecting axes and diagonals. We shall also delineate a circle. Thus we obtain a geometry of the floor area. Now by following the movements of a man over it, we get a clear demonstration of the elementary facts of its space (illustration **1**). By means of taut wires which join the corners of this cubical space, we obtain its midpoint, while the diagonal lines divide it stereometrically. By adding as many such aerials as we wish, we can create a spatial-linear web which will have a decisive influence on the man who moves about within it (illustration **2**).

Let us now observe the appearance of the human figure as an event and recognize that from the very moment at which it becomes a part of the stage, it also becomes a "space-bewitched" creature, so to speak. Automatically and predictably, each gesture or motion is translated in meaningful terms into a unique sphere of activity. (Even the "gentleman from the audience," removed from his sphere and placed on the stage, would be clothed

---

[5] In the original presentation of this lecture-demonstration, the demonstration proper began at this point. (Translator)

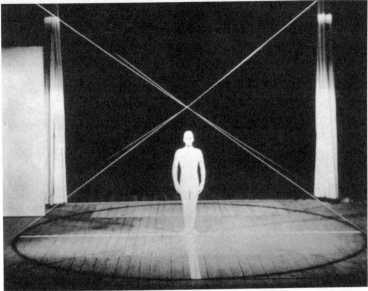

Figure in Space with Plane Geometry and Spatial Delineations.

Photograph: Lux Feininger.

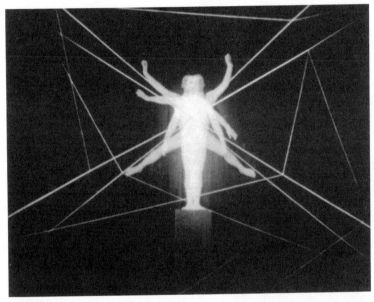

Spatial Delineation with Figure.   Photograph: Lux Feininger.

Stages in Dramatic Gesturing (Siedhoff).   Photograph: Consemüller.

From a Choric Pantomime. Photograph: Lux Feininger.

Space Dance (Schlemmer, Siedhoff, Kaminsky). Photograph: Consemüller.

Form Dance (Schlemmer, Siedhoff, Kaminsky). Photograph: Consemüller.

Gesture Dance I (Schlemmer, Siedhoff, Kaminsky).

Photograph: Consemüller.

in this magical nimbus.) The human figure, the actor, naked or in white tights, stands in space. Before him, the receptive spectator, awaiting every motion, every action. Behind him, the security of a wall; at each side, the wings for his entrance and exit. This is the situation which any person creates who instinctively steps back from a group of two or more curious spectators in order to "act out" something for them. It is the basic situation which produced the peep show. It might even be called the origin of all theatrics.

From this point on, two fundamentally different creative paths are possible. Either that of psychic expression, heightened emotion, and pantomime (illustration **3**); or that of mathematics in motion, the mechanics of joints and swivels, and the exactitudes of rhythmics and gymnastics (illustrations **5** ff.). Each of these paths, if pursued to its end, can lead to a work of art. Similarly, the fusion of the two paths can result in a unified art form. The actor is now so susceptible to being altered, transformed, or "entranced" by the addition of some applied object — mask, costume, prop — that his habitual behavior and his physical and psychic structure are either upset or else put into a new and altogether different balance. (The nature of the actor, and of the potential actor, is best revealed in the depth of the transformation of his behavior as effected by these inanimate attributes, a cigarette, hat, cane, suit, or whatever it might be.)

Light Play, with Projections and Translucent Effects.

Photograph: Lux Feininger.

Since, moreover, we are not concerned with imitating nature and for this reason use no painted flats or backdrops to transplant a kind of second-rate nature onto the stage — since we have no interest in make-believe forests, mountains, lakes, or rooms — we have constructed simple flats of wood and white canvas which can be slid back and forth on a series of parallel tracks and can be used as screens for light projection. By back-lighting we can also make them into translucent curtains or wall areas and thereby achieve an illusion of a higher order, created directly from readily available means (illustrations **8, 9**). We do not want to imitate sunlight and moonlight, morning, noon, evening, and night with our lighting. Rather we let the light function by itself, for what it is: yellow, blue, red, green, violet, and so on. ● ● ● Why should we embellish these simple phenomena with such preconceived equations as: red stands for madness, violet for the mystical, orange for evening, and so on? Let us rather open our eyes and expose our minds to the pure power of color and light. If we can do this, we shall be surprised at how well the laws of color and its mutations can be demonstrated by the use of colored light in the physical and chemical laboratory of the theater stage. With nothing more than simple stage lighting,

From a Pantomime with Figures and Translucent Walls (Lou Scheper, Siedhoff).

Photograph: Lux Feininger.

we can begin to appreciate the many possibilities for the imaginative use of color play.

We shall dress one . . . two . . . three actors in stylized padded tights and papier-mâché masks. The effect of the tights and masks together is to re-group the various and diffuse parts of the human body into a simple, unified form. The three actors will be dressed in the primary colors: red, yellow, blue. If we now assign to each of these actors a different way of walking — a slow, a normal, and a tripping gait — and if we let them measure out their space, so to speak, in time to a kettledrum, a snare drum, and wooden blocks, the result will be the "space dance" (illustration **5**). If we put certain basic forms, such as a ball, a club, a wand, and a pole, into their hands, and if we let their gestures and movements instinctively follow what these shapes convey to them, the result is what we can call "form dance" (illus-tration **6**). ● ● ● If we now provide the masks with mustaches and glasses, the hands with gloves, the torsos with stylized dinner jackets, and if we add to their various ways of walking also places to sit down (a swivel chair, an armchair, a bench) and also various kinds of sounds (murmuring and hiss-ing noises; double-talk and jabbering; an occasional bit of pandemonium;

Gesture Dance II (Schlemmer, Siedhoff, Kaminsky).   Photograph: Consemüller.

A Scene for Three (Schlemmer, Siedhoff, Kaminsky).   Photograph: Consemüller.

Musical Clown (A. Weininger).   Photograph: Consemüller.

Equilibristics (Loew, Hildebrandt, Lou Scheper, Siedhoff, Weininger).

Photograph: Consemüller.

From the Triadic Ballet by Oskar Schlemmer.
Technical production: Carl Schlemmer.
Performed in Stuttgart, Weimar, Dresden, Donaueschingen (with music for a mechanical organ by Paul Hindemith), Frankfurt-on-Main, Berlin. A dance trilogy (three parts: in yellow, rose, and black). Twelve dances, eighteen costumes. (The figurines are patented.)

Photograph: Grill.
Plate from *Körperseele* by F. Giese, Delphinverlag, Munich.

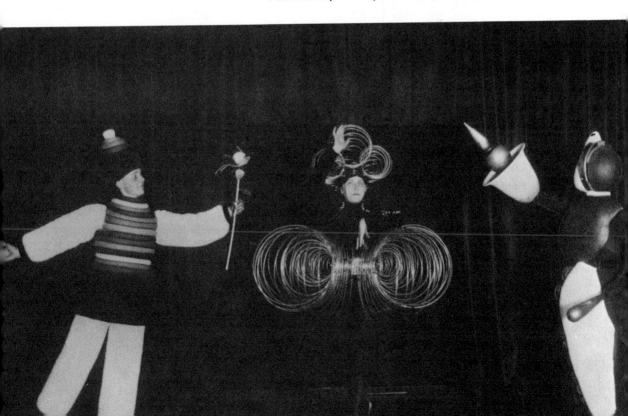

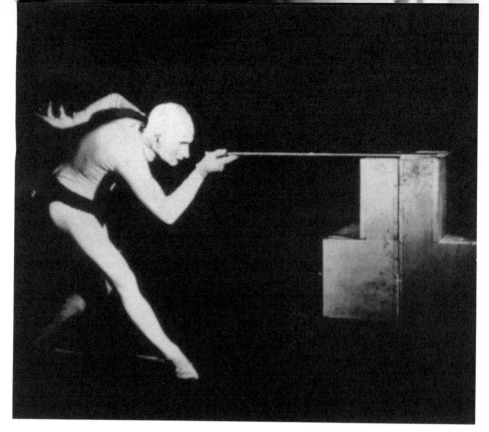

Box Play (Siedhoff).

Photograph: Hollos.

perhaps also a phonograph, piano, and trumpet), the result is what we call "gesture dance" (illustrations **7, 10**). ● ● ● The intentionally grotesque "Musical Clown" with his bare-ribbed umbrella, glass curls, colored pom-pom tuft, goggle eyes, inflated nobnose, toy saxophone, accordion chest, xylo-phone arm, miniature fiddle, funnel-shaped leg with a drum attached, gauze train, and floppy shoes, is the winsome and pathetic companion to the other three figures in a quite seriously intended quartet (illustration **12**). With these four actors as a nucleus, we now expand into a *chorus* of gray and ghostlike stereotype figures which, either individually or as a group, will demonstrate both rhythmic and dramatic patterns of motion (illustration **4**). ● ● ● Finally, we shall create for the players a universe of walls, props, and other stage equipment which can be easily transported and put up any-where (illustration **11**).

By confining ourselves to one particular area of that vast complex called the stage, to the area of pantomime and the highly disciplined chamberwork (*Kleinkunst*),

the sense of our endeavor

is to arrive at an art form which will at least try to compete with the

"legitimate" theater. This self-restriction does not come from a feeling of resignation but from the realization that by intensifying our work in such a limited area, in contrast to the ambitions of the state-supported opera and theater, we have the considerable double advantage of being free from the external restrictions of the latter (restrictions which often go far toward actually vitiating the artistic) and therefore of being able to give freer rein to imagination, invention, and technical execution. Our aim, further, is to create a different sort of play from those of others with whom we are often compared (for example, Tairoff and *The Bluebird*).[6] On the one hand, the national quality of our work is to be a native, an inherent one. On the other hand (and in no sense a contradiction), ours is a search for that which is universally valid for the creative theater. If we care to look for models, they can be found in the Javanese, the Japanese, and the Chinese theater, rather than in the European theater of today.

The point of our endeavor:
To become a traveling company of actors which will perform its works wherever there is a desire to see them.

[6] Alexander Tairoff (a pseudonym for Alexander Kornbliet, 1885–1950) was the creator in 1914 of the Moscow Kamerny Theater (*Kammertheater*) which, in contrast to both the naturalism and symbolism of Stanislavski's stage, promoted an expressive, mimetic-decorative theater style influenced by Cubism and Constructivism. The guest performances of Tairoff's theater exerted a strong influence outside Russia. Schlemmer's reference to *The Bluebird* has to do with one of the famous productions of the Moscow Art Theater under Constantin Stanislavski: Maurice Maeterlinck's *L'Oiseau bleu* had its world premier there in 1908 and, as a prized example of Symbolism on the stage, toured Europe in repertory with that company for several years; it was still being given in Moscow in 1924. (Translator)

TRANSLATOR'S NOTE

**Members of the Bauhaus stage class on the roof of the
Bauhaus building, Dessau.**

6

POSTSCRIPT AND ACKNOWLEDGMENTS

When he heard of the plan to do an English-language edition of *Die Bühne im Bauhaus,* one of the former members of that school expressed his "sympathy for the arduous task of having to render the nearly untranslatable Bauhaus prose into English." The sympathy proved not to have been misplaced.

As in any other case of translation, the words were there and each, or almost each, had its dictionary equivalent. But there was a good deal more. What needed translation was the revolutionary but curious (and in a few cases undigested) style of the Bauhaus of the early twenties. Nothing, so the credo seemed to go, was to be left without its *Gestaltung,* and language was no exception. In this document, the fourth of the fourteen Bauhaus Books, the very essence of theater was to be captured and explored and its potential as an experimental medium was to be revealed in a new way.

So, along with the ideas of Oskar Schlemmer, Laszlo Moholy-Nagy, and their students — some of them incisive indeed — were marshaled the visual attraction and shock techniques of an angular, hyperelliptical, engineered, and sparse new German manifesto style: the dashes, the dots, the exclamation points; the spaced type, the heavy type, and the capitals of Moholy's typography; the staccato paragraphing; the sketches, graphs, and photos by masters and students — and now and again a singular lyric touch or unexpected metaphor.

A steadfastly literal rendition of these essays in English proved to be sometimes vapid, sometimes meaningless, sometimes even ridiculous. Compromises were inevitable, and interpretations or interpolations through translation were necessary. But only to a certain extent, for to "be oneself" in

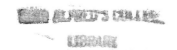

translating Schlemmer or Moholy-Nagy turned out to be almost impossible. Very often the literal translation was exactly the right thing.

The parenthetical use of the original German after the translated phrase, an easy way out in the minds of some, was made resolutely and frequently, but, in self-justification perhaps, not nearly so frequently as the temptation arose. A further attempt to retain flavor seemed to call for the incorporation of much of the original punctuation, italics, and capitalizing; and so they too remain — *auf gut Glück*. A few liberties were taken with the paragraphing. And a few notes on the text were indicated. I hope that the informed reader will be able to follow what is not easy even in the original and will approve of the method of translation and its result.

If this edition succeeds in arousing interest as a historical document and as a contribution to experimental theater even today, thanks are due in great part to those who worked over the translations and to those who assisted me in the first stages of gathering the rare and scattered illustrative materials — above all, to Dr. Walter Gropius for encouraging and facilitating the project in many ways; to Dr. and Mrs. Gropius and Mrs Sibyl Moholy-Nagy for their careful, time-consuming editing of the translation of the first Schlemmer and Moholy-Nagy essays; to T. Lux Feininger of Harvard and Ralph Pendleton of Wesleyan for suggestions in the translation of the Schlemmer demonstration lecture; to Frau Tut Schlemmer of Stuttgart, Herbert Bayer of Aspen, Colorado, Alfred H. Barr, Jr., of the Museum of Modern Art and Miss Pearl Moeller of its Division of Museum Collections, Marcel Breuer of New York City, Xanti Schawinsky of New York City, and to Curators Charles Kuhn of the Busch-Reisinger Museum at Harvard, Jay Doblin of the Institute of Design of the Illinois Institute of Technology, and Willy Rotzler of the Zurich Kunstgewerbemuseum for providing or helping locate the illustrations; and to Clinton Atkinson, and to William Ward of Wesleyan, for suggesting the project in the first place and helping it through its initial stages.

Thirty-five years have passed since this note was written and the book first published. It is gratifying that its new publisher has decided to give it a renewed lease on life. In the years since that first appearance, most of those acknowledged above have died; of the sixteen, I count only five "survivors." This hardly affects my gratitude to them expressed long ago — the accomplishments of this remarkable group of people prompt me all the more to recall and salute them again.

A. S. W.

April, 1996

Bauhaus dance in Weimar around 1922 or 1923.

PICTURE CREDITS

Many of the illustrations in this volume are identical with those in the original German book, *Die Bühne im Bauhaus* (Munich, Albert Langen Verlag, 1925). Those whose creators or photographers are unknown include illustrations on pages 11, 13, 16, 18, 19, 20, 21, 23, 24, 26, 27, 30, 32, 33, 34, 35, 36, 37, 38, 39, 41, 42, 43, 44, 45, 46, 51, 53, 54, 55, 56, 58, 59, 61, 63, 65, 66, 69, 70, 72, 75, 77, 84, 87, 89, 90, 101, 104, and 107.

Photographs by known photographers appear on the following pages: 80, 83, 93, 94, 95, 98, and 99, Consemüller; 78, 93, 94, 96, and 97, Lux Feininger; 99, Grill; 86, Hatzold; 100, Hollos; frontispiece, Strauch-Halle.

Some of these illustrations were reproduced direct from the pages of the German book, others from originals kindly supplied by their owners for this purpose. Grateful acknowledgments for the loan of pictorial materials are due to the following: Herbert Bayer, Walter Gropius, Mrs. Sybil Moholy-Nagy, Frau Tut Schlemmer, and the Museum of Modern Art, New York City.

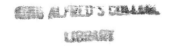